"Suffering and Sanctification"
1 Peter
Inductive Bible Study

"Yet if anyone suffers as a Christian, let him not be ashamed,
but let him glorify God in this matter."
1 Peter 4:16

"Suffering and Sanctification"
1 Peter
Inductive Bible Study
Copyright © 2012 by Morningstar Christian Chapel
Published by Morningstar Christian Chapel

Additional Copies of this book are available by contacting:

Morningstar Christian Chapel
Whittier, CA 90603
562-943-0297

Printed in the United States

Revision V1d

Suffering and Sanctification

Introduction

In his first letter, Peter writes to the scattered saints, the pilgrims in this world that were finding that it was becoming much more difficult to love and serve Jesus. The clash between the kingdom of darkness and those in the kingdom of light is inevitable. Over the centuries conflict, opposition, criticism, and persecution have been the lot of the saints. Isaiah told us Jesus would be "a Man of sorrows and acquainted with grief" (Isaiah 53:3) and John tells us that Jesus was rejected by this sinful world and by His nation as well. (John 1:10-11)

When Jesus was murdered, yet rose from the dead and later ascended, the enemies of God turned their wrath upon His followers, the church. It started early in Acts 4:1-3 as the religious leaders sought to stamp out the newly formed church. From verbal threats to physical abuse (Acts 4-5) some were arrested, threatened, and beaten.

The trial of Stephen and his death by stoning brought the first wholesale persecution of the church (Acts 6-8), which was spearheaded by a young Jewish zealot named Saul. Later King Herod would kill James, the brother of John, and arrest Peter who would be miraculously delivered by an angel the night before he too was to be beheaded.

Following Saul's awesome conversion, the church's most vicious persecutor became its most zealous missionary. Told by Ananias of how he would suffer in his ministry, Paul did indeed suffer from the moment he stepped out to preach.

Traveling through the Roman Empire he faced constant affliction and unrelenting opposition (Acts 14-27), which he mentions in nearly every epistle. As time went on, the church became more organized and so did the persecution against it.

As Peter wrote this letter, the dark cloud of the first great outbreak of official national Roman persecution was on the horizon, instigated by the insane Emperor Nero. Seeking scapegoats to divert public suspicion that he started the July 64AD fire that devastated Rome, he sought to blame the Christians whom he already hated because they would only worship Christ. As a result they were arrested, covered in wax and burned as lights in his gardens, burned at the stake, crucified, and thrown to the wild beasts.

It is in this political climate of religious persecution that Peter left two short letters to the suffering saints about standing firm in the faith through the tremendous pressure.

Since Peter does not mention the wholesale killing that began after the fire in Rome, most believe these letters were written just before the summer of 64AD, perhaps 63-64AD. This was approximately 30 years after Jesus had risen and ascended into heaven and the church had been born.

This first letter is written to a beleaguered church under siege for its faith. Up to this point, though difficult, life was much easier, and persecution was localized though sometimes severe. But now suffering greatly increased as the rages of Rome and Nero turned on the church in vengeance, and these believers needed to hear from the likes of Peter in what have been entitled "his wilderness epistles."

Peter writes of the promise of suffering and the promise of grace to endure.

> Beloved, do not think it strange concerning the fiery trial which is to try you, as though some strange thing happened to you; but rejoice to the extent that you partake of Christ's sufferings, that when His glory is revealed, you may also be glad with exceeding joy.
> (1Peter 4:12, 13)

> Yet if anyone suffers as a Christian, let him not be ashamed, but let him glorify God in this matter.
> (1Peter 4:16)

1 Peter

Perhaps we have known little, if any, of the pressures these saints faced in their daily pursuit of God. But we will indeed face the ever-present temptation to compromise our faith if it means we can avoid suffering, alienation, or difficulty serving our Lord. As the days in which we live grow darker, we must learn to walk and minister in the grace of God (1Peter 5:12) by which we are to stand daily while reaching out to the lost, despite the cost. We will learn that a true experience of God's grace does not rule out suffering for the world is lost and resistant to God.

We do not have the option to opt out of real life due to suffering. We must stand in His grace and endure, not losing our grip of the life to come!

> Therefore gird up the loins of your mind, be sober, and rest your hope fully upon the grace that is to be brought to you at the revelation of Jesus Christ;
> (1Peter 1:13)

May the Lord Jesus Christ richly bless you as you sit at His feet, seek His heart, and learn of Him! By doing so He will enable you to face any, and every, trial that comes your way with great victory!

suffering AND sanctification

Suffering and Sanctification - Outline

Lesson Index

Heavenly Stability

Remember to always begin every session of Bible Study in prayer.
It is the Holy Spirit that teaches us and reveals the truth of God's Word to us.

"However, when He, the Spirit of truth, has come, He will guide you into all truth; for He will not speak on His own authority, but whatever He hears He will speak; and He will tell you things to come. He will glorify Me, for He will take of what is Mine and declare it to you."
(John 16:13, 14)

DAY 1 – BEGIN IN PRAYER

1.   Read the entire letter of 1Peter with the following questions in mind:

What is the central message?

What was the state of the church?

What pressures were they facing?

How were they able to persevere in joy?

2.   What are your first impressions of Peter's letter, and how do you think studying it will cause growth in your walk with the Lord Jesus Christ?

3.   Record the prayer of your heart as you seek to learn about suffering and sanctification in your own life.

DAY 2 ~ BEGIN IN PRAYER

1. Read 1 Peter 1:1-5

2. Peter opens with a greeting and immediately gives his readers some good reasons why they should be rejoicing and having victory, though the trying of their faith had risen to a new level of potential cost. Who is he writing to?

How does he describe this group of people?

What important perspective does he remind his readers about that would help them withstand the harsh circumstances they were facing?

How will remembering this truth help you face the trials in your life today?

3. Peter's life is prominently displayed throughout the gospels and the early church until his miraculous delivery from death row in Acts 12:7. He is mentioned as having been present at the council meeting in Jerusalem (Acts 15), and Paul in Galatia also gives us a few other details of his travels, and his rebuke. It is believed that Peter continued his ministry in Asia Minor (Turkey) because those are the provinces listed here in his opening greeting. What do we learn about the highs and lows of the walk of this man Peter from the following references?

a. John 1:41-42

b. Matthew 14:28-32

c. Matthew 16:15-17

d. Matthew 16:21-23

e. John 18:25-27

f. John 21:15-17

g. Acts 10:9-16

4. The word apostle means **one who is sent** and was not so much a title of honor at the time as a description of purpose. Peter was **simply one who had been sent by God to share the Gospel**. Peter learned from Jesus the ministry as one of the three inner circle trainees: with James and John. Thirty years later Peter still saw his ministry as a privilege and honor from the Lord. What one word does Peter add in 2Peter 1:1 that adds to His description of himself?

Use a Dictionary of Bible Words to define the word bondservant from 2Peter 1:1.

5. Peter is writing to the **pilgrims** of the dispersion throughout Asia Minor. The word **pilgrims** refer to aliens in nationality (Gentiles), as well as, to those who have only a temporary residency here (as in all Christians because this is not our home). It is true that this life can be hard, but this is not our home! What does Hebrews 11:13-16 tell us about the hope of the pilgrims?

What does 2Corinthians 5:1-7 add to your perspective of life in this world?

6. Choose a verse from today's study to be your memory verse for the week. Record it here and begin to memorize it today!

DAY 3 ~ BEGIN IN PRAYER

1. Read 1 Peter 1:1-5.

2. According to verse 2, how does Peter describe those who were dispersed in Pontus, Galatia, Cappadocia, Asia, and Bithynia?

Peter used the word **elect**, and he follows it by three descriptive clauses. What are they?

3. The word **elect** means **chosen, selected, picked**...and we are encouraged in many places in the Bible that God has chosen us! Entire volumes and libraries have been written that attempt to reconcile the Sovereignty of God with the responsibility we have to come to Him. Both God's choosing and man's obligation to respond is clearly taught in the Bible. So both are true Biblically, and it would seem only God can fully reconcile them. What do you learn about God's choosing and invitation?

    a. John 6:37

    b. John 15:16

    c. 1 Timothy 2:3, 4

    d. Revelation 22:17

The salvation of man starts with the moving of God upon our hearts (Ephesians 2:8, 9), and He alone can receive the credit! The word **foreknowledge** tells us that God knew those who would come. He chose us beforehand, and prepared for us a life that we could walk in and serve Him. Man's responsibility is to respond to His calling. God alone has foreknowledge, but that does not mean He causes action, though He knows it and plans accordingly. This word foreknowledge is used only one other time in the New Testament. Read Acts 2:23. Did God force the actions of these men against the Lord? Did He know ahead of time that it would happen?

4. Secondly, Peter describes the **elect** as **realized by the sanctification of the Spirit**. The word sanctification (**hagios**) means **set apart** and is also the word for saint. In the present perfect tense it speaks of the ongoing work of the Holy Spirit in setting your life apart for God. What do the following Scriptures teach you about the process of sanctification?

   a. Hebrews 10:10-14

   b. 2Timothy 2:19-21

   c. 1Thessalonians 4:3, 4

5. Thirdly, this ongoing work of the indwelling Spirit of God is made evident by our obedience to God's Word. He enables us, and works in us, to transform our lives into His image. It is because of the blood Jesus shed for us that we are able to enter His presence washed from every sin. Obedience is the proof of our election – salvation. How do these Scriptures encourage you to more fully surrender and obey God's Word for your life?

   a. John 14:23

   b. 1John 2:5

6. Record your memory verse for this week, and spend time committing it to memory today. Remember the importance of hiding God's word in your heart!

DAY 4 – BEGIN IN PRAYER

1.   Read 1 Peter 1:1-5.

2.   Beginning in verse 3, Peter breaks into a long uninterrupted praise chorus that in Greek extends through verse 9. He praises God for His mercy in their lives: past, present, and future. He speaks of the wonders of salvation. List his praises from verses 3 and 4.

Record the praises of the Psalmist from the following Scriptures.

    a. Psalm 18:46

    b. Psalm 31:21

    c. Psalm 66:20

Write your own Psalm of praise! Be detailed and specific in your thanksgiving!

3.   The word **blessed** in Greek is the word for **eulogy**. It means to celebrate with words of praise or applause from lips and heart. Our understanding of our salvation should cause us to sing praises regardless of the stress of daily living. According to verse 3, what is the motive for our inheritance?

How do the following Scriptures more fully describe the reason that **God the Father of our Lord Jesus Christ** reached out of eternity to bring us salvation?

    a. Lamentations 3:22, 23

b. Psalm 86:15

c. Ephesians 2:4, 5

4. Grace is getting what we do not deserve; mercy is not getting what we do deserve because God pities us in love! Therefore, it is because God was motivated by love and mercy that we have a living hope. According to 1 Peter 1:3, 4, what act of God secures our inheritance in Christ?

Jesus died for our sins but rose to give us life! In Him we are given an abiding, living hope that depends not on our strength but on His promise. The resurrection brought new birth. God has caused us to be born again, and with our new birth, a living hope grips our hearts. How does 1 Corinthians 6:14 encourage you in your walk today?

5. How does 1 Peter 1:4 describe the inheritance that is ours by God's abundant mercy and the resurrection of Jesus Christ from the dead?

What promises do you find in the following Scriptures, and how will remembering them change how you face the circumstances of today?

a. Acts 20:32

b. Ephesians 1:11-14

c. Colossians 1:12-14

6. Can you record your memory verse without looking? If not, spend some time working on it today.

DAY 5 – BEGIN IN PRAYER

1.   Read 1 Peter 1:1-5.

Finally, not only is our future guarded, so is our present. God's power will shield and watch over us.

2.   According to verse 5, what do we learn about our eternal security in Jesus Christ?

We have an incorruptible and undefiled inheritance that will not fade away, and it is reserved for us in heaven. Not only is our future guarded, but also so is our present. We have the assurance that each and every day God's power will shield and watch over us. Use your Dictionary of Bible Words to define the word **kept** in verse 5.

3.   God is at work 24 hours a day and will get us to the end! His power ensures we will make it. How do the following Scriptures encourage you in your walk today?

a. Psalm 37: 23, 24

b. Proverbs 2:8

c. John 10:28-30

d. Romans 8:33-39

4.   We do have the responsibility to live each day by faith in Jesus Christ. He is our shield! What do we learn from Ephesians 6:16?

What amazing truth is added in Deuteronomy 33:27?

5.   Peter ends verse 5 with the phrase ready to be revealed in the last time. What do you think he meant by this phrase?

The salvation of the believer is threefold in the New Testament: it consists of **justification** – when we come to Jesus we are made just as if we never sinned – dealing with sin's past and delivering us from sin's penalty; **sanctification**, the process whereby we are daily being delivered from sin's power and hold on our lives; and finally there is **glorification**, the future aspect of salvation where we are wholly delivered from sin's presence entering into the presence of God. Salvation here in 1 Peter 1:5 speaks of that final step when we enter God's presence. What encouragement do you find in 1 John 3:2,3 about this final aspect of salvation? How will it affect your walk today?

How can you apply 2 Corinthians 4:16-18 to the circumstances you find in your life today?

6.   Record your memory verse below without looking! Can you do it? If not, keep working on it until you can!

DAY 6 – BEGIN IN PRAYER

1.   Spend today reading through the week's lesson and your answers. (Don't skip this!)

2.   How has the Lord spoken specifically to you through the lesson this week?

3.   What Scripture meant the most to you?

4.   Record your memory verse below without looking!

Salvation Assurances

DAY 1 – BEGIN IN PRAYER

1.   Read 1 Peter 1:1-12.

2.   Peter was writing in 64AD to the scattered saints living in the provinces of Asia Minor (modern day Turkey). Record an important lesson you learned from last week's study of 1 Peter 1:1-5.

How were you able to apply it in your walk this week? Be specific.

3.   Re-read 1 Peter 1:6-12.

4.   Is there a warning or a promise? Is there an exhortation or a command?

Select one to apply to your walk with the Lord this week. Which is it?

5.   Choose a verse from this portion of Scripture, and make it your memory verse for this week. Begin working on it today.

DAY 2 – BEGIN IN PRAYER

1.   Read 1 Peter 1:6-12.

2.   Peter begins verse 6 saying, **In this you greatly rejoice**… What is he referring to?

The early church was scattered throughout Asia because of severe persecution in Jerusalem. They had amazing promises of an inheritance to come, incorruptible and undefiled…reserved for them in heaven. However, they were facing a grim reality in their daily lives, and Peter writes to them, and us, about why the Lord

allows trials and how we can walk through them in victory. What do we learn about trials from verse 6?

3.   In the sure and certain promises of eternity we can **greatly rejoice**! Literally we can **jump for joy**. Our election, our position, our security in Christ is fully established. How can this truth influence how we deal with hardships in our daily life?

Peter was writing to men and women, believers in Jesus Christ, who were facing very real threats, and they would soon become deadly as Nero began his carefully orchestrated terror campaign against the church. They would need to establish a correct outlook on the trials and learn to face them with a heavenly perspective! So must we! What phrase in 1 Peter 1:6 talks about the **length** of our trials?

In the context, whatever we face for Jesus in this life is short lived or temporary. How do the following Scriptures encourage you to keep your eyes on Jesus in the midst of the trials in your life?

    a. Isaiah 54:7, 8

    b. Romans 8:18

    c. 2 Corinthians 4:17, 18

    d. 1 Peter 5:10, 11

4.   When we face trials in our lives, we have to keep our eyes on the eternal picture and spend this time, even in the difficulty, trusting the Lord. In 1 Peter 1:6, Peter includes the phrase, **if need be**...meaning if God sees purpose in trials to help us grow and allow His work to be accomplished, then we can be assured of their necessity, as well as, their brevity in our lives. According to

James 1:2-4, what is the purpose of the trials in our lives?

What does 1 Thessalonians 3:1-5 add to your understanding about the trials in your life?

5.   In 1 Peter 1:6 we learn something else about the trials we face. What do we learn about how the trials might affect our emotions?

The word **grieved** means **to be dejected, heavy-hearted, in emotional distress, or discouraged**. We are not required to act as if there is no pain, hurt or suffering involved. Rather, what we must learn is that as we respond in faith, Jesus will carry us through. How does the truth of Isaiah 43:1-3 strengthen you for the trial(s) you are facing today?

One more lesson from 1 Peter 1:6 is found in the word **various**. What does this teach us about the kinds of trials we might face?

What promise is given to you in Psalm 34:19 about sure and certain victory through the traials?

6.   Record your memory verse for this week and spend time committing it to memory today. Remember the importance of hiding God's word in your heart!

DAY 3 – BEGIN IN PRAYER

1. Read 1 Peter 1:6-12.

2. In verse 7 we are given another insight into the phrase **if need be** (v.6) which is attached to every trial God asks us to endure. What will be the outcome when we faithfully walk through hardships that our Heavenly Father allows in our lives?

What amazing promise is given to us in Romans 8:28 regarding the circumstances in our lives?

Can you remember a time when you saw this promise at work in your life? Record a few details of your praise report.

3. What further insight are we given regarding God's control in our lives and His perfect plan for making us into His image?

   a. Jeremiah 29:11-13

   b. Matthew 5:10-12

   c. Romans 5:3-5

4. It is important that we remember that God does not waste trials and suffering. There is nothing that touches our lives that isn't for good to refine our faith. What analogy does Peter use that speaks of refining?

What was Job's conclusion in this matter according to Job 23:10?

The word **tested** means to **prove**, or test **for genuineness**. It is a word that was used in assaying metals. As a certification test may prove that we are capable, so trials are designed by God to purify our faith in Him. We find out what we believe, what we will pay, and how long we will hang in there with Him. What do we learn from the following Scriptures about this testing process?

    a. Deuteronomy 8:2, 3

    b. Proverbs 17:3

    c. Malachi 3:2, 3

5.   The reality of our faith and relationship with Jesus is best seen when it is under pressure. Trials burn away hindrances, drive people to their knees, bring them to fellowship; they also challenge lethargy, lack of commitment, selfishness, worldliness, and doubt and fear. What does the parable in Mark 4:14-20 teach us about the priorities in our lives?

Peter tells us our faith in God is of far greater value than even pure gold (the most precious and highly valued metal of the day) which will perish with the world. What does he say in 1 Peter 1:7 about the mature faith that is produced by trials?

One day we will stand as a testimony of God's faithfulness and ability! How does 1 John 2:28 encourage your to draw closer to Jesus today?

6.   Record your memory verse for this week and spend time committing it to memory today.

DAY 4 – BEGIN IN PRAYER

1. Read 1 Peter 1:6-12.

2. Though we look forward to that day when we shall see Jesus face to face and honor Him, we do not need to see Him to love Him, for by faith we have already experienced His work in our lives. His Word, His Spirit, and His presence assure us He can be trusted and believed. Our walk must be a walk of faith! How does Jesus' interaction with Thomas in John 20:26-29 reveal our need to walk in faith in the midst of trials?

   What do you learn about faith and sight from these accounts recorded in the Gospel of John?

   a. John 6:35, 36

   b. John 9:35-39

3. Peter had seen Jesus. He had walked closely with Him for three years, and yet he failed Him because it is faith and not sight that brings us to the true knowledge of God. When Peter admitted that he **could not**...God enabled Him. What do we learn from the following Scriptures about this vital truth?

   a. 2Corinthians 4:18

   b. 2Corinthians 5:6-9

   c. 2Corinthians 5:16

4. Faith brings spiritual sight. Isaiah wrote that many would see but not truly understand and Jesus quoted that truth in Mark 4:12. According to Hebrews 11:1, what is the definition of faith?

Hebrews 11 is devoted to defining faith; it is not blind faith but faith proven by the Word of God and taught by the Holy Spirit, evidenced in the lives of others, and confirmed in our hearts as well. What do you learn from the testimony of John?

    a. 1 John 1:1-3

    b. 1 John 4:14

5.   According to 1 Peter 1:8, what will be the outcome in our lives when we choose to truly walk by faith and not by sight?

There is no reason for us to lose our joy seeing all we have been given and what awaits us. When we are confident that the Lord has a good and perfect plan for our lives, what is the end of our faith according to verse 9?

How does this promise affect your outlook on the trials you are facing today?

6.   Record your memory verse for this week, and spend time committing it to memory today.

DAY 5 ~ BEGIN IN PRAYER

1. Read 1 Peter 1:6-12.

2. Peter places the importance of the Old Testament Scriptures squarely before us. Sadly, many neglect their importance. Salvation is the Bible's theme: beginning in the historical books, threaded through the entire Old Testament, clearly revealed in the Gospels, lived and shared in Acts, taught in the Epistles, and concluded in Revelation. What does Peter tell us about the prophets of old?

From Moses to Malachi the prophets were fascinated with the salvation of the Lord. What does verses 10 and 11 reveal about their search?

3. The Lord used the prophets to write the Old Testament and most often they were writing things that they could not understand. The Lord was painting a picture that would come into focus when His full plan was fully revealed. What instruction did the Lord give to Daniel about his writings in Daniel 12:8, 9?

What do we learn about the ministry of the prophets from the words of Jesus in Matthew 13:16, 17?

4. What a privilege we have been given to have the full counsel of God's Word and the revelation of His plan of salvation. Record Jesus' words to the disciples as He opened their understanding to the revelation of the prophets in Luke 24:44-47.

As a reminder of the prophetic nature of the Old Testament writings, read the following prophecies regarding the coming Messiah.

    a. Psalm 22

    b. Isaiah 7:14

    c. Isaiah 9:6

    d. Isaiah 53

5. The Old Testament writers wrote to us, the church, not to themselves. Peter declares that the Gospel was taught and preached to the church by the apostles as the Holy Spirit was poured out upon them. These were truths that **even the angels desired to look into**. They are so involved in every aspect of God's work, yet according to Ephesians 3:10, how do they learn about God's plan?

The privilege of having what the prophets sought so diligently to understand, what the Holy Spirit inspired, what the apostles preached, and the angels desired to look into realized in our salvation ought to give us a constant cause to rejoice exceedingly, even in the trials, which are for a moment. Are you? If not, will you ask Him to give you an eternal view this week?

6. Record your memory verse for this week, and spend time committing it to memory today.

DAY 6 – BEGIN IN PRAYER

1. Spend today reading through the week's lesson and your answers. (Don't skip this!)

2. How has the Lord spoken specifically to you through the lesson this week?

3.   What Scripture meant the most to you?

4.   Record your memory verse below without looking!

Staying Clean in a Polluted World

DAY 1 – BEGIN IN PRAYER

1. Read 1 Peter 1:1-21.

2. Peter wrote in 64AD to the scattered saints living in the provinces of Asia Minor (modern-day Turkey). Record an important truth you learned from the last week's lesson.

How were you able to apply it in your walk this week? Be specific.

3. Read 1 Peter 1:13-21.

4. Is there a warning or a promise? Is there an exhortation or a command?

Select one to apply to your walk with the Lord this week. Which is it?

5. Choose a verse from this portion of Scripture and make it your memory verse for this week. Begin working on it today.

DAY 2 – BEGIN IN PRAYER

1. Read 1 Peter 1:13-21.

2. As Peter continues his letter that is sometimes called the "wilderness epistle" he turns from the subject of our need to walk in hope to the vital importance of walking in holiness. According to 1 John 3:2, 3, how are these two truths linked together?

suffering AND sanctification

3. Spurgeon called holiness "God's architectural design for His living temple, the church." The Greek word for **holy** is most often **hagios**, meaning **to be separated for**; in this case it means set apart solely for God and His service. When we are saved we are set apart from the world. We are at odds with their standards and goals because we live to serve God, who saved us. Peter directs our attention to the future to help us learn how to live in the present. What exhortation does he give us in verse 13?

How does this eternal view affect your attitude about today's trials?

What similar instructions are we given in the following Scriptures about our need to wait expectantly?

   a. 1 Thessalonians 5:6-8

   b. Romans 13:11-14

   c. 1 Peter 5:8, 9

4. Peter begins verse 13 with the word therefore, which refers back to the angels who are watching and the prophets who were wondering about the gospel of grace. What do you think Peter meant by **gird up the loins of your mind**?

The illustration of **girding up the loins** would have been common in Peter's day. Men wore long flowing robes that were fine until they needed to work. They would then pick them up from the hem and tuck them into the sash, or belt, to provide freedom of movement. Spiritually, how does this concept apply to the mind?

The whole idea of being girded speaks of being ready and willing to move. How is it illustrated in Exodus 12:11?

5. One solution when facing inevitable persecution is to have a mind filled with the truth that will enable you to stand through the trial without wavering. Remember, outlook determines outcome and then attitude determines action. If we are expectantly ready and waiting for Jesus' return, it is a great motivation to keep us from falling into sin. What valuable lesson do we learn from Philippians 3:13-16?

Peter writes that we must **be sober**, literally **not drunk**, and it implies being in full possession of one's faculties, or **of a sound mind**. The Lord's imminent coming ought to calm and encourage us to stay the course and to walk in victory. How are you encouraged by 1 Peter 4:7, 8?

According to verse 13, what are we to rest our hope upon when we face trials in our lives?

We must have a spiritual mindset to fully rest upon the grace of God. We must do so in anticipation of that grace being fulfilled when Jesus returns! Peter tells us that "keeping our eye" on Jesus' return will strengthen our faith and hope, even during times of terrible suffering. What promise is given in James 1:12 to the one who endures to the end?

6. Record your memory verse for this week and spend time committing it to memory today. Remember the importance of hiding God's word in your heart!

DAY 3 ~ BEGIN IN PRAYER

1.   Read 1 Peter 1:13-21.

2.   According to verses14-15, how are we to live our lives regardless of the trials we are facing?

In what manner did we live in the past?

How are we to live now that we are in Christ?

3.   It is the truth, whether we like it or not, that kids inherit the nature of their parents. The good news is that when we are born of God we inherit His nature. He is holy; therefore, we are to be holy! What do we learn from 2 Peter 1:2-4?

The amazing truth is that as His children God empowers us to obey as we submit to the indwelling Holy Spirit. How does Ephesians 2:1-3 describe the "former course" of the believer?

What amazing miracle took place according to verse 1?

How does Ephesians 4:17-19 clearly describe the nature of mankind apart from Christ?

4.   We once lived in the world as children of disobedience, and it showed. We were accurate reflections of our old nature. But when we are saved, we are given a new nature. What exhortation is found in Romans 12:1-2, and how can you apply it to your walk with the Lord today?

We are called to live in the newness of life that Jesus purchased for us with His sacrifice at Calvary. What instruction does Jesus give to us in John 14:21?

5.   According to 1Peter 1:15, **He who called you is holy**...so must we also be holy. How must this transformation show itself in our lives?

      a. Ephesians 5:1, 2

      b. Philippians 2:14-16

      c. 1Peter 2:9, 10

6.   Record your memory verse for this week and spend time committing it to memory today.

DAY 4 ~ BEGIN IN PRAYER

1.   Read 1 Peter 1:13-21.

2.   In verse 16 Peter quotes from Leviticus to show us that holiness for the saints is indeed the revealed will of God. We should be in the process of becoming

more like our Lord as He dwells in us and works in us...we are to be a spiritual transformation in progress. Record the call of God on the lives of His children from the following Scriptures.

a. Leviticus 11:44

b. Leviticus 19:2

c. Leviticus 20:7

3. **It is written** is a statement that should carry great weight for every saint! The primary question in our lives ought to be, "What does God's Word say?" What do we learn about the unchanging Word of God and its powerful influence in our lives?

a. Psalm 19:7, 8

b. 2Timothy 3:16, 17

c. Hebrews 4:12

4. The word **if** in verse 17 can be translated "**since**." Since we call Him Father, we must realize that in His holiness He is also just. He is the judge of man's behavior and works without partiality, so we must seek Him in obedience. He knows our hearts and motives, and He has redeemed us so we might live for Him. What future event ought to remind us to keep our hearts reverent before the Lord?

One day our works will be judged. This will be a family judgment as our Father looks to find good works and lives. What does God's Word teach us about this judgment of our works?

    a. Romans 14:10-12

    b. 1 Corinthians 3:11-15

    c. 2 Corinthians 5:9, 10

5. Therefore if Jesus is our Lord, we must be in the process of becoming more like Him. It may be a slow process, but we must be moving in the right direction. What does verse 17 tell us about the heart attitude needed to motivate us toward holiness?

How can you describe this **fear** in which we are to walk?

Summarize what you learn from Hebrews 12:18-29 regarding the holiness of God and the importance of godly fear.

6. Record your memory verse for this week, and spend time committing it to memory today.

DAY 5 – BEGIN IN PRAYER

1. Read 1 Peter 1:13-21.

2. We are to conduct ourselves throughout the time of our stay in fear (reverence) toward the Lord. He must always be the first priority in our lives. After all, it is He who saved us and He who will return to bring us to glory. He is holy and wants His children to be so too. He has given us His Word, warned us of His judgments, and assured us of His love. According to verses 18-21, what is the highest motive for holy living?

3. What does Peter remind us about our past?

What does he tell us about our redemption?

When was this plan ordained?

Where are we to place our faith and hope?

Why do these truths encourage your walk today?

4. We were once slaves to sin, without hope of release, and yet Jesus came and paid the ultimate price for our sins...shedding His precious blood as the Lamb without spot or blemish. What do the following Scriptures remind you about this amazing sacrifice?

    a. 1 Peter 2:22-24

    b. 1 Peter 3:18

    c. Galatians 1:3-5

    d. Ephesians 1:7

    e. Hebrews 9:12-14

How can you apply these eternal truths to the circumstances you face in your life today?

5.   This amazing redemption was no afterthought. It was not plan B on God's agenda. When was it foreordained according to 1 Peter 1:20?

Jesus' death was an appointment, not an accident! How did Peter describe His death in Acts 2:22-24?

6.   Record your memory verse for this week and spend time committing it to memory today.

DAY 6 ~ BEGIN IN PRAYER

1. Spend today reading through the week's lesson and your answers. (Don't skip this!)

2. How has the Lord spoken specifically to you through the lesson this week?

3. What Scripture meant the most to you?

4. Record your memory verse below without looking!

The Strength of His Love

DAY 1 – BEGIN IN PRAYER

1. Read 1 Peter 1:1-25.

2. Peter wrote in 64AD to the scattered saints living in the provinces of Asia Minor (modern day Turkey). Record an important truth you learned from last week's lesson.

How were you able to apply it in your walk this week? Be specific.

3. Read 1 Peter 1:22-25.

4. Is there a warning or a promise? Is there an exhortation or a command?

Select one to apply to your walk with the Lord this week. Which is it?

5. Choose a verse from this portion of Scripture and make it your memory verse for this week. Begin working on it today.

DAY 2 – BEGIN IN PRAYER

1. Read 1 Peter 1:22-25.

2. Remember the context! Peter tells us how we should live in order to survive the difficulties of this world's opposition. God calls us to walk in His love, and He places a premium on church life, body life, and God's love in our hearts. According to verse 22, what took place in our souls, and how will it be revealed in our lives?

2.   Peter takes his readers back to the starting point of their Christian lives when they had **purified their souls by obeying the truth** of God in the power of the Spirit. In the Old Testament there were many washing ceremonies designed to illustrate the need for God to cleanse us before we could ever come into His presence. What do we learn from the following Scriptures regarding this ceremonial cleansing?

     a. Exodus 19:10

     b. Numbers 8:7 & 21

     b. Isaiah 1:16-18

3.   Jesus spoke of this need for cleansing at the Last Supper in John 13:8-10. What do we learn from Peter's encounter with Jesus?

When we come to the Lord and are saved, we immediately experience a changed heart, and then a life-long washing process begins. The Holy Spirit begins to daily cleanse our minds, our motives, our outlooks, and our goals. He changes us from within; not as religion, which seeks to make outward changes. What more can we learn about this transformation process from Philippians 2:13?

How does Paul describe this work of the Spirit in 1 Corinthians 6:9-11?

4.   The unconverted do not have the ability to love with God's love. How is this truth made clear in the following Scriptures?

     a. John 5:42-43

b. 1 John 3:10

c. Luke 11:42

5.   We obeyed the truth of God as revealed by His Spirit and were saved; as a result of His indwelling Spirit, we began to have a loyal family affection for one another. Use a Dictionary of Bible Words to define the two different Greek words, which are both translated **love** in verse 22.

Peter says that brotherly **love (Greek - philadelphia)** was evident among the churches. The word **sincere** means **without wax, or genuine**. When we are born again the Holy Spirit moves into our hearts and gives us an even greater capacity to love with a higher love – **agape** – God's love. What commandment is found in John 13:34-35?

6.   Record your memory verse for this week, and spend time committing it to memory today. Remember the importance of hiding God's word in your heart!

DAY 3 – BEGIN IN PRAYER

1.   Read 1 Peter 1:22-25.

2.   As Peter continues speaking about the absolute necessity of **agape love** being the controlling factor in the life of the believer, what exhortation is given in verse 22b?

How does 1 John 3:14-18 clearly describe and define **agape love**?

3. Peter calls the church to **love one another fervently with a pure heart**. The word **fervent** is a physiological term that speaks of extending one's reach as far as possible. **Agape love** is a love displayed by God for man and one that comes to dwell in us as the Holy Spirit sets up residence in our hearts. It is an exercise of the will in obedience to God that is not moved by beauty, desirability, or the deserving state of the one loved, but rather the noble intention of the one who loves. Read about it in action on your behalf. Selah!

    a. John 3:16

    b. Romans 5:8

    c. 2Corinthians 5:21

    d. 1John 4:9, 10

4. What exhortation does Peter add in 1Peter 4:8 about our need to **fervently love**? How specifically can and will you apply this in your life this week?

How does 1Corinthians 13:4-8a describe the daily actions of God's agape love?

5. Remember Peter is writing to the church that is facing increasingly severe persecution. Only the agape love of God will be able sustain us as a body under pressure. How does Galatians 5:16 & 22-25 express this powerful love of God?

The agape love of God is seen when we treat others the way God treats us. In the case of those Peter is addressing it may very well have taken the form of great cost. How does Acts 2:42-46 show us the practical aspect of agape love in the church?

6. Record your memory verse for this week and spend time committing it to memory today.

DAY 4 – BEGIN IN PRAYER

1. Read 1 Peter 1:22-25.

2. So much has been said about the importance of body ministry within the church. We are all one but with many members. Each member is equally important; some are much less visible, but all are of equal value to the Lord. Peter tells us we are to **love one another**. There are many statements in the New Testament that fall under the category "to one another or unto one another". What do we learn from these vital exhortations in the book of Romans?

    a. Romans 12:5

    b. Romans 12:10

    c. Romans 12:16

    d. Romans 13:8

    e. Romans 14:19

    f. Romans 15:7

g. Romans 15:14

3. What other commands do we find in the following Scriptures?

    a. Galatians 5:13

    b. Galatians 6:2

    c. Ephesians 4:2

    d. Ephesians 5:21

    e. 1 Peter 5:5

4. **Personal**: The above is a list of agape love in action. Is there an area that needs improvement in your love?

5. **Personal**: Will you ask the Lord to change your heart as you surrender your will to the power of His Holy Spirit in you? Write out your prayer to Him.

6. Record your memory verse for this week, and spend time committing it to memory today.

DAY 5 — BEGIN IN PRAYER

1. Read 1 Peter 1:22-25.

2. Peter ends this section by saying to the believers that only when they have been born again will they have the capacity to love as God loves. According to verse 23, how does this new birth process take place?

What do we learn about the life changing, nature transforming power of the Word of God?

   a. Proverbs 30:5

   b. Romans 10:17

   c. Ephesians 6:17

   d. Hebrews 4:12

3. This agape love is so vital to the church and its witness to the world that Satan longs to destroy it. What are his motives and his methods?

   a. Proverbs 6:16-19

   b. 2Corinthians 2:9-11

   c. John 10:10

4. The seed of God's love that was planted in our hearts is not some perishable seed but one that lasts forever. It is the Word of God. Peter quotes from Isaiah 40:6-8. What does it say?

How does the truth of His unchanging Word help you to better face the hard issues in your life today?

5. The saint has been changed by God through His Word and the work of the Holy Spirit in our lives. The changes are permanent, and this love is to be a permanent part of our new nature. However, this love must be practiced daily and chosen in obedience. How does John 13:34, 35 challenge you in obedient love today?

6. Record your memory verse for this week, and spend time committing it to memory today.

DAY 6 – BEGIN IN PRAYER

1. Spend today reading through the week's lesson and your answers. (Don't skip this!)

2. How has the Lord spoken specifically to you through the lesson this week?

3. What Scripture meant the most to you?

4. Record your memory verse below without looking!

Temples of the Living God

DAY 1 – BEGIN IN PRAYER

1. Read 1 Peter 1:1-2:10.

2. Peter was chosen by the Lord to write two letters of hope and encouragement to a church being assaulted by Nero and Rome. He wrote them in the summer of 64AD when Nero burned down Rome and sought to blame it on the Christians. Record an important truth you learned from last week's lesson.

How were you able to apply it in your walk this week? Be specific.

3. Read 1 Peter 2:1-10.

4. Is there a warning or a promise? Is there an exhortation or a command?

Select one to apply to your walk with the Lord this week. Which is it?

5. Choose a verse from this portion of Scripture and make it your memory verse for this week. Begin working on it today.

DAY 2 – BEGIN IN PRAYER

1. Read 1 Peter 2:1-10.

2. At the end of chapter 1 Peter reminds us of God's amazing agape love that can be exercised by his kids, those who have been born of God and have the Holy Spirit dwelling in them. Now he tells us it is our choice whether we love or not! In these first ten verses how does the Lord describe the church?

When the pressure and heat are turned up through trial and tribulations, being in the company of the saints is awesome and is the place to find His love in action as we await the coming of our Lord. We must actively resist the flesh and the divisions it can bring in sin, and we must run to God and allow His Word to change us and make us more like Jesus. What word begins 1 Peter 2:1? What does it refer to?

3.   What direction (command) is given in verse 1?

We are commanded to **lay aside**...it means **to put these things off by choice**. It is a command, and it means that we need to do it now! Peter gives us five sins of discord and distrust that can hinder this walk of love we should find amongst the saints. Use a Dictionary of Bible Words to define these sins.

     a. Malice

     b. Deceit

     c. Hypocrisy

     d. Envy

     e. Evil Speaking

4.   What do the following Scriptures teach us about our personal responsibility in laying aside, or putting off, sin?

     a. Hebrews 12:1-3

     b. Colossians 3:8-10

c. James 1:21-22

5.　Malice is evil wishes against another, and is associated with our thought life. Deceit means to catch with bait and speaks of deception with words. Hypocrisy is deceit in behavior. Envy desires another's place and position while often also wishing evil on them. Evil speaking is defaming the character of another through slander. What must be the motive for the choice we make to obey God's command to lay aside sin?

a.　Ephesians 4:31, 32

b.　Colossians 3:12, 13

c.　Romans 12:20, 21

6.　Record your memory verse for this week and spend time committing it to memory today. Remember the importance of hiding God's word in your heart!

DAY 3 – BEGIN IN PRAYER

1.　Read 1 Peter 2:1-10.

2.　Verse 2 begins with the word as – it is a comparison word, a simile. As believers, what are we to be like?

How would you describe a newborn baby that's hungry at 2AM?

In like manner, as believers we should have that same desire and longing for the Word of God. Only the pure milk of the Word and nothing else will fill the desires of our heart. We must desire God's Word first and foremost; it is only here we find life. What do we learn about the sufficiency of God's Word?

      a. Psalm 19:7-10

      b. Psalm 119:9-11

      c. Psalm 119:130

      d. Ephesians 4:11-15

      e. 2Timothy 3:15-17

3.   In verse 2, Peter uses the phrase **pure milk of the Word**. It is used in 1Corinthians in a negative sense to speak of a lack of maturity and of much division in the body. Remember here it is a simile that describes the craving hunger of a nursing child for his mother's milk. What other great illustration is found in Psalm 1:1-3 that reminds us of the absolute necessity of feeding on **the pure milk of the Word**?

Record the declarations of two men whose lives were totally dependent upon the Word of God.

      a. Job 23:12

      b. Jeremiah 15:16

4. There are no shortcuts to spiritual growth; we must daily feed the spiritual man! Sadly, far too many churches today are laying aside the Word and are exchanging it for things that cannot bring eternal life. What exhortation did Paul give to Timothy in 2Timothy 2:15 regarding his relationship to the Holy Word of God?

5. Verse 3 says **if indeed**...meaning **since or after all;** it is not a question but a statement of fact. What have we tasted about the Lord?

Since taste precedes craving, it follows that if we have tasted of the Lord's grace, we will long to have more, and as we more fully rely on His grace, we will be willing to extend His grace to others. How might you extend His grace to someone in your life this week?

6. Record your memory verse for this week, and spend time committing it to memory today.

DAY 4 – BEGIN IN PRAYER

1. Read 1 Peter 2:1-10.

2. Peter's second analogy turns from a child's craving to comparing the church to a building under construction. We are the dwelling place of God on the earth. How does Peter refer to Jesus in verse 4?

How does the Lord introduce this analogy through Moses and the children of Israel in Exodus 17:5, 6?

Jesus is the Rock upon which our faith is built. What do we learn about the Rock from 1Corinthians 10:1-4?

3. According to 1 Peter 2:4, what happened to this Living Stone?

What more do we learn about this plan of redemption?

    a. Psalm 118:22

    b. Matthew 21:33-46

Man's opinion of Jesus is that He is not worthy to follow, to believe, or to trust. The nation of Israel had rejected Him because He did not match their expectation of the Messiah. Though the nations would refuse Him and the world would reject those who follow Him, what is the truth about Jesus Christ as stated in 1 Peter 2:4?

How is this truth illustrated in Matthew 3:13-17?

4. Jesus is called the Living Stone. According to verse 5, how is the believer who follows Him described?

God no longer dwells in a temple built with hands; He lives in the hearts of those who believe in Him. In the Old Testament the priests could only come from the tribe of Levi, and specifically, they were sons of Aaron. In the New Testament it is the privilege of every saint to be a **spiritual house, a holy priesthood, to offer up spiritual sacrifices acceptable to God through Jesus Christ**. What do we learn about this holy calling from the following Scriptures?

    a. 1 Corinthians 6:19, 20

    b. Ephesians 2:19-22

5.   We are to offer **spiritual sacrifices acceptable to God**. What might be an example of these sacrifices?

How do the following references add to your answer?

   a. Jeremiah 33:11

   b. Philippians 4:18

   c. Hebrews 13:15, 16

6.   Record your memory verse for this week, and spend time committing it to memory today.

DAY 5 – BEGIN IN PRAYER

1.   Read 1 Peter 2:1-10.

2.   In verse 6, Peter offers strong Scriptural support that those who follow Jesus will cause the world to make a choice about Who He is. There are only two camps, and the dividing line between them is whether or not they share God's estimation of Jesus. The dividing line is marked by the Living Stone, this one not laid with human hands. Peter was quoting the Isaiah 28:16, what promise is given to those who believe on Him?

What does 1 Corinthians 3:9-11 add to your understanding of the Living, Foundation Stone?

3. To the believer, Jesus is of the highest importance; He is precious, for without Him we perish. To see the value of food we must be hungry, of a doctor we must be sick, of a Lord and Savior we must see our sin and our need for grace and forgiveness. A choice is required! It must be an individual decision! Either He is to you the Chief Cornerstone, and you obediently surrender your life, or He is a stone of stumbling and a rock of offense. Think about your choice as you read the following Scriptures.

    a. Acts 4:11, 12

    b. Romans 9:31-33

    c. 1 Corinthians 1:23-25

Personal: In which camp do you dwell? Today is the day of salvation!

4. Peter tells us the disobedient will refuse the Word, but in contrast the believer has an amazing calling. What four phrases does 1 Peter 2:9 use to describe the believer?

    1.

    2.

    3.

    4.

What are we supposed to proclaim? Why?

But you are a chosen generation...the word **generation** in Greek is the word for **race, nationality, or descent**. What does 2Corinthians 5:17 say about the family history of the believer?

What do Revelation 1:6 & 5:10 say about the future of the believer?

5. In verse 10, Peter quotes from the book of Hosea where the Lord prophesies of Israel's future promises. Included is the promise that knowing God intimately will also come to the Gentiles. Read Hosea 2:23. What is the central theme of the book? What is the context of this promise?

Slowly and carefully read Ephesians 2:4-9. How does the unchanging truth of God's Word change the way you will act and react today?

6. Record your memory verse for this week, and spend time committing it to memory today.

DAY 6 – BEGIN IN PRAYER

1. Spend today reading through the week's lesson and your answers. (Don't skip this!)

2. How has the Lord spoken specifically to you through the lesson this week?

3. What Scripture meant the most to you?

4. Record your memory verse below without looking!

In the World, Not of It

DAY 1 – BEGIN IN PRAYER

1.   Read 1 Peter 1:1-2:17.

2.   Peter was chosen by the Lord to write two letters of hope and encouragement to a church being assaulted by Nero and Rome. He wrote them in the summer of 64AD when Nero burned down Rome and sought to blame it on the Christians. Record an important truth you learned from last week's lesson.

How were you able to apply it in your walk this week? Be specific.

3.   Read 1 Peter 2:11-17.

4.   Is there a warning or a promise? Is there an exhortation or a command?

Select one to apply to your walk with the Lord this week. Which is it?

5.   Choose a verse from this portion of Scripture and make it your memory verse for this week. Begin working on it today.

DAY 2 – BEGIN IN PRAYER

1.   Read 1 Peter 2:11-17.

2.   In our text this week we discover important details on how we, as the children of God, should live in this world in order to be effective witnesses to the unbeliever. How does Peter describe the believer in verse 11?

Use a dictionary of Bible words to define the following words from 1 Peter 2:11.

   a. Sojourners

   b. Pilgrims

3.   As **sojourners** we are to be **in** the world, but as **pilgrims** we are not to be **of** the world. We are children of the Lord who are away from home but who are heading back. What do we learn from Hebrews 11:13-16 regarding being a sojourner and a pilgrim?

How does 2Corinthians 5:1-7 give added insight into the fact that this world is not home and we are not citizens in it?

How did Jacob describe his long life on this earth according to Genesis 47:9?

4.   There is no doubt that the body of Christ is out of step with the world and that God never intended us to fit in. Like traveling to a different country and having to deal with currency conversion, languages, and societal practices that are unfamiliar to us...so the church in the world no longer relates to life on the physical plane or fleshly level, but sees itself as a vessel through whom God will reach the world. According to 2Corinthians 5:18-21, what is your role in this ministry to the world?

In our Lord's prayer for the church in John 17:15,16, what is His request for the believer?

5.   The Lord, through Peter, helps us avoid compromising with sin while not retreating from those we are sent to reach. At the same time, He reminds us of the opposition we are certain to face. How does this tough fisherman Peter

address the struggling church in 1 Peter 2:11?

Reminding us of our status as beloved children of the Lord, what does Peter entreat us to do?

How do the following Scriptures speak to the importance of the church staying pure and separate from the sin of the world?

    a. Romans 12:1, 2

    b. Romans 13:12-14

    c. Galatians 5:16-18

    d. Ephesians 4:1-3

6.   Record your memory verse for this week and spend time committing it to memory today. Remember the importance of hiding God's word in your heart!

DAY 3 – BEGIN IN PRAYER

1. Read 1 Peter 2:11-17.

2.   The church must maintain a holy walk with the Lord if we are to be effective in removing the common excuses the unbeliever has for not seeking Jesus. What is Peter's exhortation in 1 Peter 2:12?

Use a dictionary of Bible words to define the word **conduct** in verse 12.

Why must our conduct be honorable among those in the world?

What do we learn from these two tragic examples of one man and one chosen nation that did not keep their **conduct honorable**?

    a. 2Samuel 12:13-14

    b. Ezekiel 36:20-23

3.   The word **honorable** in 1Peter 2:12 means **beautiful, excellent, attractive, appealing to the eye**. We are to live in the world in such a way that our example attracts their attention and leaves a mark, an impact, that draws them rather than gives them an excuse to turn away. How are Jesus' words in Matthew 5:14-16 an encouragement to you today?

4   We need to remember that even when we walk in obedience to the words of our Lord many will not be interested in hearing, and some will be strongly opposed to the Lord whom we serve. How does 1Peter 2:12 remind us of the opposition we are certain to encounter?

Opposition will certainly come! It is a guarantee! We should not be surprised or discouraged when the Gospel message we share is rejected. Use the following truths as a reminder to persevere and to not waver in your walk with the Lord.

    a. Matthew 10:24-26

    b. John 15:18-21

c. 1 John 3:13

d. Proverbs 29:27

5. Peter tells us that our best defense against accusation is not words to counter the lies but rather beautiful lives lived so that others can truly see the love of Jesus. What practical instruction is given to us in Philippians 2:14-16? How do you plan to put it into practice today?

As a last reminder for today, what were Jesus' words to Saul on the road to Damascus found in Acts 9:5?

Personal: If someone is persecuting you for your love and obedience to Jesus, Who are they really persecuting?

6. Record your memory verse for this week and spend time committing it to memory today.

DAY 4 ~ BEGIN IN PRAYER

1. Read 1 Peter 2:11-17.

2. We have learned that we are to abstain from the world's sin, yet live in the world as witnesses to the lost, and to be ambassadors of Christ who boldly declare His love. We are to be detached yet still very much engaged as a witness and light. In verses 13-14 Peter begins to talk about the believer's responsibility to government and rulers, and to the law of the land. As believers, we must submit and be great citizens even though we are only here on a visitor's pass! What command is given to us?

What does the word **therefore** in verse 13 refer to?

Romans 13:1-5 gives us valuable details about the governments and leaders that are set in place to rule over nations. What do we learn?

3. Use a dictionary of Bible words to define the word **submit** in 1Peter 2:13.

Why are we to submit ourselves to the laws and leaders of the land?

What does 1Timothy 2:1-4 add that reminds us to daily submit ourselves to those in authority over us? Why?

To submit is more than just to obey; it speaks of a willingness to comply and to follow those who have been placed in a position of authority. We must be willing to submit because we understand that the Lord has placed them in their position. What does Proverbs 21:1 teach us about the ultimate sovereignty of God?

4. We are to submit to every ordinance of man **for the Lord's sake.** We are to honor Him and to be a vessel for His work of evangelism. It matters not the type of government we live under (monarchy or democracy, or evil dictator). We are to submit, for God's will is that we shine for Him. What do we learn from Psalm 75:6, 7?

It was Artaxerxes (an unbelieving king) who sent Ezra back to Jerusalem to restore and rebuild the Temple. What do you learn about this miracle from Ezra 7:25-28?

Another king presumed that he was mighty in all the earth until the LORD dealt with his pride. Read Daniel 4, what was the conclusion of the matter according to King Nebuchadnezzar?

5.   In 1 Peter 2:14 we find a second reason that we must obey the ordinances of man. Sometimes we find in the Scriptures that God allows a nation to have wicked rulers for the purpose of dealing with its wicked people. We see this in the history of Israel and its captivity in Babylon. According to 1 Peter 2:15, what is the ultimate reason for our obedience to the governments that God has ordained?

Pay careful attention to the instruction in verse 15. To criticize our government or its overseers is to speak evil against God who placed them in authority. It is through our honest lives and well doing, coupled with prayer that God desires to silence the ignorant comments of foolish men and to remove their excuses for not turning to Jesus in faith. God's plan is that we live consistent godly lives. What can you learn from Peter's example in Acts 4:7-13 when his faithful service got him arrested?

6.   Record your memory verse for this week, and spend time committing it to memory today.

DAY 5 – BEGIN IN PRAYER

1.   Read 1 Peter 2:11-17.

2.   It is important that we keep in mind that Peter was writing this from the context of a government and emperor who had literally gone mad! We are to live obediently, reverently, prayerfully, and not critically. A question arises, "What if the government orders those things God specifically disallows or prohibits that which God specifically demands?" What are you to do? What is your Biblical support?

How does Daniel 3:13-18 support your answer?

What were the circumstances in the early church recorded in Acts 4:19-20 and 5:29 that demanded disobedience to the command of the ruler?

3. The submission to authority is not bondage for we are God's servants, and this is His will. We are free to obey Him! No one is freer than a believer in Jesus, and with the truth comes a warning in 1 Peter 2:16. What is that warning?

What do we learn from Galatians 5:13 about this liberty and our responsibility to use it appropriately?

How did Paul describe his use of his liberty in relation to his need to protect a weaker brother or sister in 1 Corinthians 7:9-13?

4. Liberty misused is like a mighty river overflowing its banks and causing much destruction. The blessing of the river becomes a curse. It is the same with a believer who refuses to submit to authority; his life becomes an ineffective witness and looks no different than the world. How does Peter describe the believer in 1 Peter 2:16?

Use a dictionary of Bible words to define the word **bondservants**.

Look at the common use of the term **bondservant** amongst the apostles.

a. Titus 1:1

b. James 1:1

c. 2 Peter 1:1

d. Jude 1:1

What do we learn about the bondservant from the following Scriptures?

a. Ephesians 6:5, 6

b. Colossians 3:22

5. Peter tells us that the servants of the Lord will serve their Master freely! They have chosen to follow Him; they have surrendered their will to His; they have offered their lives as a living sacrifice; therefore, according to 1 Peter 2:17, how then shall they live?

We are to honor **all** people! Not just the saints. Not just our friends. Not just our neighbors. We are to honor **all** people. We are to reverence them and value them highly. They need a good witness in order to be saved. Jesus died for them, so we must treat them with respect and dignity. How does Matthew 5:44-48 encourage you in obeying 1 Peter 2:17 today?

6. Record your memory verse for this week, and spend time committing it to memory today.

DAY 6 – BEGIN IN PRAYER

1. Spend today reading through the week's lesson and your answers. (Don't skip this!)

2. How has the Lord spoken specifically to you through the lesson this week?

3. What Scripture meant the most to you?

4. Record your memory verse below without looking!

Following Jesus' Example

DAY 1 ~ BEGIN IN PRAYER

1.   Read 1 Peter 1-2.

2.   Peter was chosen by the Lord to write two letters of hope and encouragement to a church being assaulted by Nero and Rome. He wrote them in the summer of 64AD when Nero burned down Rome and sought to blame it on the Christians. Record an important truth you learned from the last week's lesson.

How were you able to apply it in your walk this week? Be specific.

3.   Read 1 Peter 2:18-25.

4.   Is there a warning or a promise? Is there an exhortation or a command?

Select one to apply to your walk with the Lord this week. Which is it?

5.   Choose a verse from this portion of Scripture and make it your memory verse for this week. Begin working on it today.

DAY 2 ~ BEGIN IN PRAYER

1.   Read 1 Peter 2:18-25.

2.   In this portion of 1 Peter we are given a simple lesson to learn. It is a practical lesson with concrete directions from the heart of God. It speaks of how we can bring the Lord glory and be a witness for Him in the midst of the increasing hostility in which we live. It is totally contrary to the world's view of flexing your muscle and getting your way. What exhortation is given to us in 1 Peter 2:18?

Building upon 1 Peter 2:11-17, Peter reminds us that submission is a powerful tool and that by following Jesus' example, we can honor our God and be used by Him. The instruction in verse 18 is not addressed to someone else. It is an exhortation to every believer. Have you considered yourself to be a servant today?

3. **Servants be submissive to your masters**…here the call is to suffer though we have not done anything to deserve it! What does a servant do and how does he live according to the following Scriptures?

    a. Mark 10:42-45

    b. John 13:14-17

    c. Romans 6:18-22

    d. Galatians 5:13

    e. Galatians 6:2

4. Slavery was a way of life in the Roman Empire: nearly 60 million men, women, and children served in all kinds of positions, and most often they served for life. Though slavery itself is a horrendous mistreatment of man that cannot be supported, neither Jesus, Peter, nor Paul ever counseled the church to protest or oppose the practice; but rather they encouraged the slave to use that place of submission to shine and manifest God's love. Today we can apply these instructions to our service at work, in the community, and in our churches. What do we learn from the following verses about service?

    a. Ephesians 6:5-8

    b. 1 Timothy 6:1

c. Titus 2:9-10

5. It might be easy to serve under the authority of a good and kind master (employer), but if that is not the case, how are we to serve?

The word **harsh** in verse 18 means **unjust, cruel, crooked**. If your boss is a tyrant, how are you to serve?

Re-read and review the instructions found in Philippians 2:14-16 from last week's lesson. Make it your practice as you walk with the Lord today!

6. Record your memory verse for this week, and spend time committing it to memory today. Remember the importance of hiding God's word in your heart!

DAY 3 – BEGIN IN PRAYER

1. Read 1 Peter 2:18-25.

2. Peter spoke of the action that we must take in verse 18. What does verse 19 teach us about the attitude with which we are to serve?

Use a dictionary of Bible words to define the word **commendable** in verse 19.

Peter tells us that it is a token of grace at work in us, a sign that God lives in our hearts, which causes us, or allows us, to serve even the harshest of masters, bosses, or leaders in our lives. This behavior brings forth the acknowledgement and approval of God. The same Greek word (**charis**) is used three times in Luke 6:32-36, what do we learn about how we are to walk?

3. It is important that we are mindful that our lives are to be a living witness for the Lord. This is God's will and His desire for our lives; and this is the motive by which we must serve those who are kind to us and, even more importantly, how we respond when we suffer wrongfully. How are Jesus' words in Matthew 5:10-12 a comfort and an encouragement to you?

What instruction are we given in James 1:2-4, and how will you apply it to your life today?

Record James 1:12, and carry it with you as a promise today!

4. If we are willing to allow God to orchestrate our lives, then we must be willing to die to ourselves in the process, let Him fight our battles, and make things right in His sight. What are we told in verse 20 about suffering patiently?

The word credit in verse 20 means **praise or glory**. There is no benefit to our witness or to God's honor if we suffer patiently for things we have brought on ourselves. We deserved it; we got it; no light here! Yet, when suffering is unwarranted and unfair because we've done well, this is commendable (**grace**). His grace is displayed in you, and it honors Him! According to Romans 12:1, 2, how are we to live?

Why will obeying this command make our lives shine so brightly in this world?

5. What amazing truth is revealed to us in 1 Peter 2:21? As believers, what are we called to do?

Peter tells us it is in unjust suffering that the grace of God is put on its most effective display! Yet far too often, we avoid this area because it costs too much and because it demands faith and death to self. How do the following Scriptures speak to our calling to follow in Christ's footsteps?

a. Mark 8:34, 35

b. Philippians 1:27-29

c. Philippians 2:5-8

6. Record your memory verse for this week, and spend time committing it to memory today.

DAY 4 – BEGIN IN PRAYER

1. Read 1 Peter 2:18-25. (No skipping this!)

2. **Because Christ also suffered for us, leaving us an example, that we should follow in His steps**...think about it...what does it mean to you personally? How will it change your responses to unjust and harsh treatment today?

Use a Dictionary of Bible words to define the word **example** in verse 21.

3. We are to compare any suffering we might have to face as a Christian against what Jesus endured for us. According to Philippians 3:8-12, what was Paul's summation of the cost of his walk with the Lord?

What exhortation is given to us in Ephesians 5:1, 2?

How will this act of **walking in love** express itself in our lives?

    a. Ephesians 4:32

    b. Colossians 3:12, 13

    c. 1 Peter 1:15, 16

    d. 1 John 4:11, 12

4.   Peter continues to compare our trials with Jesus' sacrifice by quoting several verses from Isaiah 53. Read this chapter slowly, and spend time considering its amazing prophetic truths. Record a few details of this sacrifice made on your behalf.

Personal: Record a prayer of praise and thanksgiving to the Lord for this unspeakable gift of salvation.

5.   What does 1 Peter 2:22 tell us about Jesus' nature?

How does 2 Corinthians 5:21 encourage you in your walk today?

6.   Record your memory verse for this week and spend time committing it to memory today.

DAY 5 — BEGIN IN PRAYER

1.   Read 1 Peter 2:18-25.

2.   What does verse 23 tell us about the perfect nature of Jesus our Lord?

Record Isaiah 53:7. How will following Jesus' example change your walk with the Lord today?

3.   How do the following Scriptures illustrate Jesus' unjust suffering?

    a. Luke 22:64, 65

    b. Matthew 27:39-50

When He was reviled, He did not revile in return; when He suffered, He did not threaten…what did He do instead?

Personal: What do you do under similar circumstances?

4.   We are told in verse 23 that Jesus trusted Himself to Him who judges righteously. What clear direction are we given for dealing with harsh, unfair treatment?

    a. Matthew 5:38-44

    b. Romans 12:17-19

c. 1 Thessalonians 5:15

Rather than retaliating, according to Luke 23:34, what did Jesus do?

5.   According to 1 Peter 2:24, **Jesus, bore our sins in His own body on the tree**. Why?

Talk about unfair! He was sinless! He died that we might obtain righteousness! He died so that we could obtain power over sin and be able to live a righteous life serving Him. By His sacrifice we were healed. We were like sheep going astray, but the Lord intervened and drew us to Himself. The word **stripes** speak of a wound that bleeds. By His suffering we have forgiveness, but what a cost! By our submission, the world has a witness, also at a cost! It is not easy but it will be well worth it when your submission saves souls. What exhortation must we heed in Hebrews 12:1-3 if we are going to shine brightly for Jesus?

What is added in Galatians 6:9?

6.   Record your memory verse for this week, and spend time committing it to memory today.

DAY 6 – BEGIN IN PRAYER

1. Spend today reading through the week's lesson and your answers. (It's important!)

2. How has the Lord spoken specifically to you through the lesson this week?

3. What Scripture meant the most to you?

4. Record your memory verse below without looking!

68

The Power of Submission

DAY 1 – BEGIN IN PRAYER

1. Read 1Peter 1:1-3:7.

2. Peter was chosen by the Lord to write two letters of hope and encouragement to a church being assaulted by Nero and Rome. He wrote them in the summer of 64AD, the same year Nero burned down Rome and sought to blame it on the Christians. Record an important truth you learned from last week's lesson.

How were you able to apply it in your walk this week? Be specific.

3. Read 1Peter 3:1-7.

4. Is there a warning or a promise? Is there an exhortation or a command?

Select one to apply to your walk with the Lord this week. Which is it?

5. Choose a verse from this portion of Scripture and make it your memory verse for this week. Begin working on it today.

DAY 2 – BEGIN IN PRAYER

1. Read 1Peter 3:1-7.

2. We have learned how submission works as a witnessing tool that shines brightly in a dark world of self-indulgence, and that we are to follow Jesus' example of how to respond when others treat us unfairly. What instruction is given in verse 1?

Use a dictionary of Bible words to define the word **submissive** in verse 1.

3. The word **likewise** in verse 1 tells us that this instruction to wives is **in the same manner** as his word to us as citizens, slaves or employees, and as Jesus' example of submitting to the Father's care – **committing Himself to Him who judges righteously**. So likewise...re-read 1 Peter 2:13-25, how can these principles be applied in a godly manner in the life of a woman who is a wife?

Submission reflected the relationship of God's people to the world in which they lived, which brought many unfair situations: torture from Nero, slavery in the culture, false arrest, accusations, a mock trial, scourging and the crucifixion of our Lord; in each illustration a heart of submission brought victory. In context, the same response of submission, in order to gain fruit and victory, is now applied to the home life of those who know God...beginning with the wife (1-6) and then with the husband as well (7). To whom is a wife to be submissive? Why?

What instruction is found in the following Scriptures regarding submission in marriage?

a. Ephesians 5:22-24

b. Colossians 3:18

4. A wife is to be submissive to her **own** husband. The word means to **voluntarily and continuously place yourself underneath, to rank under in file**. This is not pressure from others or from without; it is a personal, individual choice that is a decision of the heart to bring glory and honor to the Lord. Our flesh naturally resists any authority, which is why Peter has said this will be such a witness...the new man has already submitted to Jesus. What more do we learn about this quality of submission to authority?

a. Matthew 8:8-10

    b. Ephesians 5:18-21

    c. Philippians 2:4-8

In terms of structure and function, God establishes different responsibilities for each individual. In terms of spiritual equality, there is no difference in the eyes of the Lord. What promise of hope is given in 1 Peter 3:1 regarding the fruit of a submitted life in a marriage?

Note that unequally yoked marriages are forbidden in God's Word. To willfully enter into such a relationship is not proper. How is this truth clearly stated in 2 Corinthians 6:14-16?

5.   Peter instructs the wife who has an unsaved husband not to go the way of the world in response to the flesh, but rather to walk in love and submission to him for this is the will of God. When she loves him and submits to him, she can trust God to soften her husband's heart. How do the following exhortations encourage you in your walk today whether your spouse is saved or not yet saved?

    a. 2 Corinthians 3:1-3

    b. Matthew 5:16

The best approach in sharing the love of Jesus is not through words but through our life, sharing only as the Holy Spirit leads! What does 1 Corinthians 7:12-16 add regarding the amazing power of a believer's life submitted to the Holy Spirit?

6.   Record your memory verse for this week, and spend time committing it to memory today. Remember the importance of hiding God's word in your heart!

DAY 3 – BEGIN IN PRAYER

1.   Read 1 Peter 3:1-7.

2.   According to verse 2, what is it about the conduct of the submissive wife that will bring about spiritual change in the life of the unbelieving husband?

Use your dictionary of Bible Words to define the following words.

     a. Observe

     b. Chaste

     c. Conduct

     d. Fear

3.   It is very clear that the world carefully watches the actions of those who say they know the way of life. We are to live in a manner that represents our Lord Jesus Christ so that those who do not yet know Him will clearly see His love shining through our lives. Genuine godliness impresses the heart of the lost. How do the following Scriptures encourage you in your walk with the Lord today?

     a. 1 Peter 1:15-19

     b. Philippians 1:27

c. 1 Timothy 4:12

d. 2 Peter 3:11

4.   What further instruction is given to the wife in 1 Peter 3:3?

According to verse 4, what is it that will shine so much brighter than the gold and fancy clothing?

Peter is not speaking against outward adornment, or outlawing it in any manner; rather he is emphasizing that real beauty that has an eternal effect is that of the heart. How does 1 Timothy 2:9, 10 describe this beauty of the heart?

5.   Women who love and serve the Lord are to be clothed **with the incorruptible beauty of a gentle and quiet spirit**. What does this description mean to you?

Read and record Proverbs 31:30. How does this truth affect the priorities in your life?

6.   Record your memory verse for this week, and spend time committing it to memory today.

DAY 4 ~ BEGIN IN PRAYER

1.   Read 1 Peter 3:1-7. (No skipping this – it is important!)

2.   Peter tells us that it is an absolute necessity that the hidden person of the heart be revealed! This voluntary, loving life of submission is a powerful tool in the hands of the Lord to reach and transform the hardened heart of the

unsaved husband. It doesn't mean a wife cannot, or should not, share her views or opinions in the home, but as she submits her heart to Jesus, miracles can take place in her home. What examples does Peter use to make his point in verses 5 and 6?

What type of women is Peter speaking about?

How did they adorn themselves?

3. God has given us amazing examples of real women of faith. They were certainly not perfect, but through trial and hardship they learned to depend upon the sure and certain Word of God. Read about Sarah's encounter with an impossible promise in Genesis 18:11-15 and Genesis 21:5-7. How does this fulfilled promise encourage you in your walk today?

What does Hebrews 11:11 teach us about Sarah?

4. Peter tells us, **in former times, the holy women who trusted God also adorned themselves with submission.** A woman's greatest strength is her relationship with the Lord. This is a very important principle – that women would trust God for the sake of their husbands, whether they are believing or unbelieving – and it applies across the board. Let's review.

a. Hebrews 13:17

b. Ephesians 5:21

c. Philippians 2:3-5

d. Colossians 3:12-14

5.   What two instructions or conditions does Peter give to the wife in 1 Peter 3:6?

What do you think he means by **if you do good?**

One major way that a wife can do good toward her husband is to protect him by not speaking evil of him and by loving him as God does. What do the following Scriptures teach us that will keep us from falling into sin with our words?

a. Psalm 37:30

b. Ephesians 4:29

Also, we must be careful not to give way to fear or worry that our doing good may never make a difference, wondering if God will ever work. There is no heart too hard, no soul unreachable. Remember the LORD'S words to Sarah. Re-read and record Genesis 18:14a.

6.   Record your memory verse for this week, and spend time committing it to memory today.

DAY 5 – BEGIN IN PRAYER

1. Read 1 Peter 3:1-7.

2. What instructions are given to husbands in verse 7?

What word in verse 7 connects this direction to the husbands with the main principle of submission beginning in 1 Peter 2:13?

3. Verse 7 begins **likewise**, or in the same manner. It says the husband must learn to submit to the Lord and to the needs of his wife. He must submit in his life, patience, care, and support, knowing that it is his responsibility to be the high priest of his home. What instructions are given in Ephesians 5:25-33 regarding God's perfect plan for marriage?

How is the husband to love?

Why is he to love in this manner?

4. 1 Peter 3:7 Peter highlights three areas of submission that are often neglected by a husband. They are consideration, chivalry, and communion. What instruction is given about each?

    a. Consideration

    b. Chivalry

    c. Communion

Use a dictionary of Bible Words to define the following words from verse 7.

   a. Understanding

   b. Honor

   c. Heirs

5.   The husband is to dwell with his wife with understanding. He must know her and know her well. He must learn to communicate with her and listen to her words and her heart. He must honor her as the **weaker vessel**. It is a comparative term. If she is **weaker**, he is at his best **weak**. He must remember that they are **heirs together of the grace of life**. She is the daughter of the Lord and the heir of grace and needs to always be treated as such. What more do we learn about marriage and God's perfect plan?

   a. Genesis 2:21-25

   b. Matthew 19:3-6

What further instruction is given to the husband in Colossians 3:19?

Since we began the discussion about submission back in 1 Peter 2:13, do you realize there has been no talk of rights, only of responsibilities? Each is to contribute faithful submission so God might bless! Submission is a tool given to us by the Lord so that we can reach the lost, secure the wayward, and shine as lights in this dark world. Take a peek ahead; Peter will revisit this important topic. What direction is given to us in 1 Peter 5:5?

How specifically can you apply it to your walk with the Lord today?

6.   Record your memory verse for this week, and spend time committing it to memory today.

DAY 6 – BEGIN IN PRAYER

1.   Spend today reading through the week's lesson and your answers. (It's important!)

2.   How has the Lord spoken specifically to you through the lesson this week?

3.   What Scripture meant the most to you?

4.   Record your memory verse below without looking!

Pursuing Peace By Submission

DAY 1 ~ BEGIN IN PRAYER

1. Read 1 Peter 1:1-3:12.

2. Peter was chosen by the Lord to write two letters of hope and encouragement to a church being assaulted by Nero and Rome. He wrote them in the summer of 64AD, the same year Nero burned down Rome and sought to blame it on the Christians. Record an important truth you learned from last week's lesson.

How were you able to apply it in your walk this week? Be specific.

3. Read 1 Peter 3:8-12.

4. Is there a warning or a promise? Is there an exhortation or a command?

Select one to apply to your walk with the Lord this week. Which is it?

5. Choose a verse from this portion of Scripture and make it your memory verse for this week. Begin working on it today.

DAY 2 – BEGIN IN PRAYER

1. Read 1 Peter 3:8-12.

2. In this week's lesson we will study the conclusion of Peter's teaching on the powerful witness of submission and how it applies to the Body of Christ; in particular our relationships with one another. What five-part command is given in verse 8?

    1.

    2.

    3.

    4.

    5.

3. As born-again believers who have been given the Holy Spirit to empower our lives, our submission to His will enables us to obey God. Religion demands but cannot provide the power to change behavior. We have been given a new heart and a new spirit to enable us to obey God's Word. In verse 8, Peter says, **finally**...and he issues a five-part command. What does he mean by the phrase **be of one mind?**

The word translated **one mind** is **homophron** in Greek and it means **harmony, like-minded, akin to, or in unity**. Therefore, as God's people we should hold the same thoughts, attitudes, and values together with the Lord when it comes to fellowship, life in this world, and submission to one another. Out of the 12 times this same Greek word – **homophron** – is used in the book of Acts, it is translated as in one accord 10 times. How do the following references help us to understand Peter's command in verse 8?

    a. Acts 2:1

    b. Acts 2:46

    c. Romans 15:5, 6

    d. Philippians 2:5-8

4.   What is Peter's second command to the submitted church in 1 Peter 3:8?

Use a Dictionary of Bible Words to define the word **compassion**.

How does the use of this word in Hebrews 10:32-34 help to show the meaning of this direction to us? How have you seen this compassion at work in your life this week?

The word translated **compassion** means **sympathy**. It is the sharing in the feeling of another, whether we agree with them or not. It is the decision to stand looking at life through their eyes, from their position, to walk a mile in their shoes. True compassion requires true understanding! The body of Christ must submit to one another in sympathy. This word is used again in Hebrews 4:15, how does this truth encourage your walk today?

5. What is Peter's third command in 1 Peter 3:8 regarding the believer's responsibility to live in submission?

The Greek word for **love** is **philadelphos**. It speaks of brotherly love or family commitment. Peter has mentioned this need to **love as brothers** twice before. What direction did he give then?

    a. 1 Peter 1:22

b. 1 Peter 2:17

What direction does Romans 12:10 add concerning brotherly love?

6. Record your memory verse for this week and spend time committing it to memory today. Remember the importance of hiding God's word in your heart!

DAY 3 – BEGIN IN PRAYER

1. Read 1 Peter 3:8-12.

2. Continuing with the five-part command of submission, what is the fourth direction given to us in verse 8?

How would you describe a tenderhearted person?

The word in Greek is **eusplagchnos**. It literally means to be of **strong bowels** because in the days Peter wrote it was thought that emotions sprung from the bowels or stomach because of how they made one feel. How did Paul use this term to encourage the Ephesian saints in Ephesians 4:31-32?

The heart of the believer needs to be soft and tender especially in an age when we are so bombarded with images, news, and stories that can leave us cold and unfeeling. Everybody faces those times when we have been taken advantage of, let down, or even rejected by those we trust. The natural tendency is to build a huge wall to avoid the pain. What completely opposite instruction are we given in 1 Corinthians 13:7 and 8a?

3. Lastly, what is the fifth part of this commandment of submission according to 1 Peter 3:8?

Finally, as believers submitted to one another in love, we are to be **courteous**. The word means **friendly, or kind**. Overall, be kind to others as the Lord is kind to you! According to Galatians 5:22-23, how can you accomplish this in your life?

What is added in the following Scriptures, and how will you apply it to your relationships today?

    a. Ephesians 4:2

    b. Colossians 3:12

4.   In verse 9 Peter continues on this same topic of submission. What instruction, that is absolutely opposed to the attitude of the world, does he give to the submitted believer?

Unlike the natural man who can be very vengeful and unwilling to turn the other cheek, the church knows that the best way to shine is by blessing! What do we learn from the following commands of submission to the church?

    a. Matthew 5:43-48

    b. Romans 12:20-21

5.   Instead of returning evil for evil or reviling for reviling, what are we to do?

Why are we to take this action?

The Lord doesn't pay evil for evil...or we would all be long gone. Instead He only requires us to give out what we have received. Notice verse 9 says, that we **may inherit a blessing**. An inheritance is not earned, it is given freely; therefore, we ought to give freely the blessing that we have been blessed with. Use the following command of submission in Romans 12:14-19 as the guide by which you interact with others today. Record your prayer asking the Lord to make you the child He desires you to be so that you can more effectively reach the lost with His love.

6.   Record your memory verse for this week, and spend time committing it to memory today.

DAY 4 – BEGIN IN PRAYER

1.   Read 1 Peter 3:8-12. (No skipping!)

2.   How is the promise of future blessing described in verse 10?

Since Peter has been speaking of the submission of the believer, how does submission apply to this promise?

Peter's quote is from Psalm 34:12-16. What do you learn from this Psalm that will strengthen your walk with the Lord this week?

3.   Remember the audience to whom Peter was writing. Most likely they were not "enjoying life" under the heavy hand of Nero; however, the world's idea of the good life is far removed from God's! Yet in Jesus we can have that rewarding, rich, fulfilling life only as we follow His word regarding our speech and pursuits. There is a certain connection between the words of our mouth and the attitude of our heart. How does Psalm 19:12-14 make this connection, and what is the Psalmist's prayer?

Peter deals with two basic issues in the life of the believer, and both have to do with our control of our tongues. What strong statement does James make in James 1:26 about this needed area of submission?

4. Use a Dictionary of Bible Words to define the following words from verse 10:

    a. Evil

    b. Deceit

In the battle to put on the new man, the area of taming the tongue ranks near the top as one of the most difficult members to surrender to God. What does James 3:1-12 tell us about this battle?

5. The heart is exposed by the words of the mouth. The world would long to change the fruit – the words or speech, but it is only God that can transform the root – the heart. What does Matthew 12:33-37 say about this conflict?

One day we will give an account for the content of our heart as evidenced in our speech. Let's return to a portion of Scripture we looked at earlier this week and determine the solution to this sin of speaking evil and deceit. The problem is sin, and the solution is submission to the control and power of the Holy Spirit. What instructions are given in Ephesians 4:29-5:2? How will this change the way you walk and talk today?

How will the command of Colossians 3:16, 17 encourage your obedience and guard your lips today?

6. Record your memory verse for this week and spend time committing it to memory today.

DAY 5 – BEGIN IN PRAYER

1. Read 1 Peter 3:8-12.

2. What further instruction are we given in verse 11?

The word translated **turn** means to **avoid, or stay out of the way**. Peter moves from the importance of not speaking evil to the need for every believer to stay away from anything that is evil. We are to avoid evil at all costs. How does Genesis 39:7-13 illustrate the perfect offensive action that is required in the life of the submissive, obedient child of God?

3. In order to have victory in our walk with the Lord, we must be certain not to linger or remain in a place where temptation will cause us to struggle and fall. What four words of action are found in 1 Peter 3:11?

What more do we learn about our responsibility to walk in righteousness and obedience?

     a. Proverbs 3:7

     b. Proverbs 16:17

     c. Galatians 6:10

     d. 1 Timothy 6:18

     e. 3 John 1:11

4. We are to **turn away from evil and do good**; and we are to **seek peace and pursue it**. We are to be peacemakers in the Body of Christ. We are to live in peace, seek it in the sense that it is not always readily found; yet when it is, we must pursue it. What do the following Scriptures teach us about our responsibility to pursue peace?

    a. Romans 12:18

    b. James 3:17, 18

5. How does 1 Peter 3:12 motivate us to walk in submission?

God is watching, and not only does He see our actions, He knows our thoughts and is keenly aware of our motives. Read Psalm 139. How will these truths make a difference in how you walk today?

6. Record your memory verse for this week, and spend time committing it to memory today.

DAY 6 – BEGIN IN PRAYER

1. Spend today reading through the week's lesson and your answers. (It's important!)

2. How has the Lord spoken specifically to you through the lesson this week?

3. What Scripture meant the most to you?

4. Record your memory verse below without looking!

Drawing Attention to Jesus

DAY 1 – BEGIN IN PRAYER

1. Read 1 Peter 1:1-3:22.

2. Peter was chosen by the Lord to write two letters of hope and encouragement to a church being assaulted by Nero and Rome. Persecution was on the rise, and the church was suffering tremendously because of their faith in Jesus Christ. Record an important truth you learned from last week's lesson.

How were you able to apply it in your walk this week? Be specific.

3. Read 1 Peter 3:13-22.

4. Is there a warning or a promise? Is there an exhortation or a command?

Select one to apply to your walk with the Lord this week. Which is it?

5. Choose a verse from this portion of Scripture, and make it your memory verse for this week. Begin working on it today.

DAY 2 – BEGIN IN PRAYER

1. Read 1 Peter 3:13-22.

2. Peter has been teaching about submission as the way to reach the lost and to minister one to another within the body. He now focuses on the difficult side of submission – including how to live godly lives when we are unfairly treated, falsely accused, manipulated and used. What instruction does 1 Peter 3:13, 14 give us regarding how we are to respond?

Remember the context of the entire passage we are studying. According to 1 Peter 2:21-25, Who is our example in submission and why was He willing to die?

3. These verses are straightforward, and the logic and wisdom in them are absolute. The lesson is that suffering for doing right brings life to others; suffering for being sinful is simply justice. Therefore, if suffering occurs, the question we need to ask ourselves is, what is the cause, and what is the effect? What encouragement and strength do you find in the following Scriptures about the suffering in our lives?

    a. Luke 6:22, 23

    b. Philippians 1:27-29

    c. Isaiah 41:10-13

According to 2 Corinthians 12:10, what was Paul's response to the trials in his life?

4. Peter continues with a rhetorical question that says that most people will respond to goodness and love with joy; most will not strike back when they hear and see Jesus' love in us. However, 1 Peter 3:14 gives us the exception to this truth. How should you respond when you suffer for righteousness' sake?

Note the words **but even if you should suffer for righteousness' sake**...If it should occur in our walks with Jesus, Peter reminds us to see it as a blessing. What do we learn from Matthew 5:10-12 & 16 about this blessing?

Peter calls for us to make a conscious decision to not allow fear or worry to invade our walks and service in a hostile world. He tells us to cheer up, look up, and have an eternal perspective. Read the account of the Apostles in Acts 5:27-42. What was their response to the threats and beatings?

Peter quotes from Isaiah 8:11-13, what are we told in this amazing prophecy? How can you apply this to the hard circumstances in your life?

5.   According to 1 Peter 3:15, what must we do instead of being fearful and afraid, or discouraged and brokenhearted?

Our Christian faith will make no sense to the world, and our Christian lives will be unfruitful until we set apart our lives for the Lord. What does it mean to **sanctify the Lord God in your hearts**?

Jesus is to be at the Master control of our lives, calling all the plays and making all the choices. As we learn to obey Him, the fear of man will be replaced with a complete trust in God. The result will be a peace that will have those around you asking how they can have what you have. Are you prepared to give an answer? What would you say?

6.   Record your memory verse for this week, and spend time committing it to memory today. Remember the importance of hiding God's word in your heart!

DAY 3 – BEGIN IN PRAYER

1.   Read 1 Peter 3:13-22.

2.   Peter was writing to a people who had little to rejoice about and even less hope for the near future; and yet, as children of God they had an eternal peace that stood in marked contrast to the world. Our life and response in submission is the best testimony we can possibly have. Peter encourages us to live our faith in such a manner that many will desire to know **why** and **how** we can have such amazing hope. According to the following verses, what is our responsibility for preparation?

a. Matthew 10:16

b. Romans 1:16

c. 1 Corinthians 1:22-24

d. Colossians 4:5, 6

e. 2 Timothy 3:16, 17

3.   According to 1 Peter 3:15,16 how are we to approach the lost?

To be an effective witness to those who recognize the eternal hope in our lives, we must approach them **in meekness and fear, having a good conscience**. Will you and your message always be well- received?

Record 1 Peter 2:19-20 as a reminder and an encouragement in your walk today.

4.   Christians cannot live double, or secret, lives. We are called to be authentic, transparent, and genuine as we live for Jesus in this world. According to 1 Peter 3:16, why is a **good conscience** essential in the life of the believer?

There is a suffering that comes from doing the wrong thing and it causes the light in our lives to be hidden from view. Peter constantly repeats this truth so that we will remember to walk in a manner that brings glory and honor to our Lord. What will he add later in 1 Peter 4:15 that will help you in your walk today?

5.   What do we learn about suffering from 1 Peter 3:17?

We must learn to trust in the Sovereignty of our Lord in knowing that it is God's will that we face suffering for doing what is right and pleasing in His sight. The fact that we suffer for doing right graciously will cause those who are watching to see our faith and response to the trials, and then they will wonder how it is possible... and we can boldly tell them. What does Romans 8:28 teach us about the outcome of suffering?

In Genesis 50:20, how does Joseph's response to his brothers encourage you to walk uprightly today in the face of unfair treatment?

Lastly, according to 1 Peter 3:18, how does our willingness to suffer for righteousness' sake bring us a closer identity with our Lord and Savior?

6.   Record your memory verse for this week, and spend time committing it to memory today.

DAY 4 – BEGIN IN PRAYER

1.   Read 1 Peter 3:13-22.

2.   It seems that verses 19-22 are a topical parenthesis in Peter's letter. He diverges from his topic as he begins to think about Jesus and His work for us. He returns to his topic in chapter 4:1. Notice in these verses that Peter tells us we were saved because Jesus was willing to suffer for us and that, in so doing, He now sits in authority over all powers that exist. According to verse 19, what did Jesus do by the power of the Holy Spirit after His death?

In the Old Testament the word **sheol** is translated **grave, death, and hell**. It is to the **spirits in prison** or those souls who died without the knowledge of the Savior that Christ went to preach. In the New Testament the word is **hades**. Prior to Jesus' death, all the souls of men went to this place (sheol or hades) - both believers and unbelievers. What does Psalm 16:10 teach us about this moment in history?

3. How does Matthew 12:39-40 speak about this time when Jesus **preached to the spirits in prison**?

What more do we learn from the following Scriptures about the period of time between Jesus' death and resurrection?

   a. Matthew 16:21

   b. Matthew 17:22, 23

   c. Matthew 27:63, 64

   d. John 2:19-21

4. Jesus gave a very insightful teaching in Luke 16:19-31 that speaks about this place of Hades. Read this account of the rich man and Lazarus, and record the main details of their story.

What do the following Scriptures add to your understanding of this time when Jesus **preached to the spirits in prison**?

   a. Isaiah 61:1

   b. Ephesians 4:8-10

5. The word translated **preached** (kerrasso) in 1Peter 3:19 is not the usual word for preaching. This word means to **proclaim or declare**. Jesus went to Abraham's bosom declaring His victory over sin and death for them, and then He led those in captivity to freedom in heaven. How does Paul celebrate this truth in Colossians 2:13-15?

6. Record your memory verse for this week and spend time committing it to memory today.

DAY 5 – BEGIN IN PRAYER

1. Read 1Peter 3:13-22.

2. In 1Peter 3:20, Peter refers to the longsuffering of God in the days of Noah; for 120 years, he waited patiently for the people to turn from their sins as they daily observed the ark being built. Yet with all His waiting, only 8 escaped. What do we learn about the longsuffering of the Lord from the following Scriptures?

    a. Psalm 86:15

    b. Romans 2:4

    c. 2Peter 3:9

    d. 2Peter 3:15

3. Even with such limited success, God waited patiently in the days of Noah. Knowing this to be true ought to encourage us when we feel our unjust suffering is not bearing fruit fast enough or in insufficient quantities. Remember God waited for 8! What encouragement do you find to walk patiently today?

a. 1 Timothy 1:15-17

b. 2 Timothy 4:2-5

4. Peter uses the time of Noah and the flood as a symbol. The phrase **saved through water** refers to the flood in looking back to Noah's day and then forward to baptism. In the flood, God's judgment fell on man and his flesh and wickedness. In the New Testament, baptism identifies with the death of our flesh and subsequent rise to walk in newness of life by His Spirit, Who is given to those who trust in Jesus Christ as their Lord and Savior. How is this truth described in Romans 6:3, 4?

5. What clarifying statement does he make in 1 Peter 3:21 regarding water baptism?

Remember the context! The church was under increasing persecution, and it might have appeared that God was not in control. They faced major rejection and discouragement, and like Noah, they had to trust the Lord and consider the fruit in the manner that God did in Noah's day. Peter is not saying that we must be baptized to be saved. Rather, we must rest in Jesus' death and resurrection to cleanse us and deliver us from sin. As the floodwaters cleansed the earth, so baptism is an **antitype** or symbol that separates us from the wickedness in the world today. How can you compare your life in Christ to Noah in the ark?

How does Hebrews 2:8, added to these final verses of 1 Peter 3, remind you that you are safe and secure in Christ regardless of the hardship you face in this present world?

6. Record your memory verse for this week, and spend time committing it to memory today.

DAY 6 – BEGIN IN PRAYER

1.   Spend today reading through the week's lesson and your answers. (It's important!)

2.   How has the Lord spoken specifically to you through the lesson this week?

3.   What Scripture meant the most to you?

4.   Record your memory verse below without looking!

Serious Times Require a Serious Witness

DAY 1 – BEGIN IN PRAYER

1. Read 1 Peter 1:1-4:9 (Read it as a personal letter written to you. Don't skip this!)

2. Peter was chosen by the Lord to write two letters of hope and encouragement to a church being assaulted by Nero and Rome. Persecution was on the rise, and the church was suffering tremendously because of their faith in Jesus Christ. Record an important truth you learned from last week's lesson.

How were you able to apply it in your walk this week? Be specific.

3. Read 1 Peter 4:1-9.

4. Is there a warning or a promise? Is there an exhortation or a command?

Select one to apply to your walk with the Lord this week. Which is it?

5. Choose a verse from this portion of Scripture, and make it your memory verse for this week. Begin working on it today.

DAY 2 – BEGIN IN PRAYER

1. Read 1 Peter 4:1-9.

2. Using the word **therefore** in verse 1, Peter refers back to what he wrote in Chapters 1-3. What exhortation does he give us in this first verse?

Since Christ suffered for us in the flesh...He did so to save us, to forgive us, to reach and redeem us, for our benefit and our eternal hope. The word **arm** means **to equip**. Use a Dictionary of Bible Words to define the word **mind** in verse 1.

3. Peter asks us to look at the attitude and outlook of Jesus as He faced suffering. We are to equip ourselves with that same determined understanding when we face suffering in our lives. How do Jesus' words in John 15:18-24 encourage and challenge you in your walk today?

How do the following words of our Lord serve as a comfort and reminder?

a. Matthew 5:11, 12

b. Luke 6:22, 23

4. According to the following Scriptures, what are some of the things that characterized Jesus' attitude toward suffering?

a. Philippians 2:5-8

b. John 15:13

c. Hebrews 12:2

d. Ephesians 1:18

e. 1 Peter 2:23

5. Therefore, when we face suffering in our lives, we are to do so with the mind of Christ. Jesus was willing to suffer tremendously so that we could have eternal access. Are you willing to be His vessel for that same purpose?

Peter adds a comparison here in verse 1. In the battle we face in this world we must die to our flesh, which is the equivalent of **ceasing from sin**, because sin always has its root in **self**. How does this concept compare to the attitude of the world in which we live?

What does Galatians 5:24, 25 teach us about this painful practice of obedient living?

6. Choose a verse from this portion of Scripture, and make it your memory verse for this week. Begin working on it today.

DAY 3 – BEGIN IN PRAYER

1. Read 1Peter 4:1-9.

2. When we give our lives to the Lord Jesus Christ, God breaks the power of our old sinful nature and puts us on a new road. What does 2Corinthians 5:15-18 teach us about this new life in Christ?

This new road leads us to a new mission in Christ. What are we to no longer do according to 1Peter 4:2?

3. How are we to accomplish this work in our lives?

    a. Ephesians 4:22-24

b. Colossians 3:1-5

What details are we given about the **lusts of men** in Ephesians 4:17-19?

4.　From the time we trusted Jesus as our Lord and Savior, we committed to live the **rest of our time** according to the **will of God**. According to the following Scriptures, what is the will of God for His children?

a. Ephesians 6:6

b. 1 Thessalonians 4:3

c. 1 Thessalonians 5:18

d. 1 Peter 2:15

What does 1 John 2:17 teach us about the one who does the will of God?

5.　How does Peter describe the former years in the life of a believer in Christ in 1 Peter 4:3?

Why do you think he uses a phrase like **our past lifetime**?

How is this an encouragement to you when the enemy reminds you about sins of your past lifetime?

6. Record your memory verse for this week and spend time committing it to memory today. Remember the importance of hiding God's word in your heart!

DAY 4 – BEGIN IN PRAYER

1. Read 1 Peter 4:1-9.

2. It is amazing that the Lord speaks of our past as **our past lifetime**. It carries the meaning of being closed and finished. What declaration does Paul make in Philippians 3:13, 14, and how can you apply his exhortation to this truth in 1 Peter 4:3?

How did the saints in Hebrews 11:13-16 deal with their **past lifetime**?

3. Peter clearly reminds us that we have spent enough time in the world to learn that the world lives for sin, and sin has horrible rewards. It does not, and cannot, satisfy! How does he define the worthless ways of the world in 1 Peter 4:3?

What is added in the following Scriptures about the empty ways of the world that lead to death?

    a. Ephesians 2:1-3

    b. Ephesians 4:17-20

    c. Galatians 5:19-21

    d. Colossians 3:5-7

Write a prayer of praise and thanksgiving if you can confidently declare this to be **your past lifetime**!

4.   What does 1 Peter 4:4 say about how your former "party mates" think and speak of the change in your behavior?

Use a Dictionary of Bible Words to define the word **dissipation**.

It is at this point that some believers try to court the affections of the world and seek to win favor again with those separated from them by their new birth in Christ. What exhortation and warning is given in the following Scriptures?

     a. 2 Corinthians 6:17, 18

     b. John 12:42, 43

5.   The truth is that those who pass judgment on you for your faith will one day give an account of their actions. Judgment is sure and certain! What is the difference between the judgment of the believer and the unbeliever?

     a. 2 Corinthians 5:10

     b. Revelation 20:11-15

6.   Record your memory verse for this week and spend time committing it to memory today.

DAY 5 – BEGIN IN PRAYER

1.   Read 1 Peter 4:1-9.

2.   In verse 6 Peter points back to those saints who had died (maybe some recently in the wave of persecution from Nero) physically but who had lived for Christ and had been witnesses who were willing to pay the price for being faithful. When the Gospel is preached it will indeed cause separation; we have certainly been forewarned of this truth. What do we learn?

   a. Matthew 10:17-22

   b. Matthew 24:9-13

3.   In light of us one day having to answer to God and stand before Him, Peter speaks of the Lord's coming for us as very near. What is his instruction to us in verse 7?

Throughout the Bible we are counseled and encouraged to wait with anticipation for the Lord's soon return. All the New Testament writers lived with this conviction. **Do you**? How do the following Scriptures remind us to walk in anticipation, waiting for His soon coming?

   a. Romans 13:12-14

   b. Philippians 4:5

   c. Hebrews 10:24, 25

   d. James 5:8, 9

    e. 2 Peter 3:9-11

4. According to 1 Peter 4:8, what should be our highest priority? Why?

How do the following Scriptures describe God's love?

    a. John 15:12, 13

    b. 1 Corinthians 13:4-8a

5. What parallel instruction is given to us in 1 Peter 4:9?

Why do you think Peter included this instruction?

How can you specifically apply it in your walk with the Lord today?

6.   Record your memory verse for this week, and spend time committing it to memory today.

DAY 6 – BEGIN IN PRAYER

1.   Spend today reading through the week's lesson and your answers. (It's important!)

2.   How has the Lord spoken specifically to you through the lesson this week?

3.   What Scripture meant the most to you?

4.   Record your memory verse below without looking!

Serving the Body, Suffering in the World

DAY 1 – BEGIN IN PRAYER

1. Read 1 Peter 1:1-4:19 (Read it as a personal letter written to you. Don't skip this!)

2. Peter writes to the church about its present challenge of persecution, the work of reaching the lost in the process, and the hope that awaits them in the presence of God. Persecution was on the rise. The church was suffering tremendously; therefore, Peter writes with hope and encouragement. Record an important truth you learned from last week's lesson.

How were you able to apply it in your walk this week? Be specific.

3. Read 1 Peter 4:10-19.

4. Is there a warning or a promise? Is there an exhortation or a command?

Select one to apply to your walk with the Lord this week. Which is it?

5. Choose a verse from this portion of Scripture, and make it your memory verse for this week. Begin working on it today.

DAY 2 – BEGIN IN PRAYER

1. Read 1 Peter 4:10-19.

2. Peter continues his letter by encouraging the persecuted saints to remain actively involved in serving within the church. What is his exhortation in verses 10 and 11?

Use your dictionary of Bible Words to define the word **gift** in verse 10.

3.   Read the following Scriptures and make a list of the spiritual gifts God gives to the believer.

    a. Romans 12:6-8

    b. 1Corinthians 12:4-11

    c. Ephesians 4:11-13

4.   What instruction did Paul give to Timothy regarding the use of the gifts God had given him?

    a. 1Timothy 4:14

    b. 2Timothy 1:6, 7

5.   There is some distinction made between these gifts of grace and the natural talents which are given by God to all men, saved or not. What does verse 10 tell us regarding our use of these gifts of grace?

Spiritual gifts are for serving, not for feeling superior or for status, not for drawing attention to ourselves or for personal benefit. What do we learn from the following verses about our responsibility to **one another**?

    a. John 13:14

    b. John 13:34, 35

c. Romans 12:10

d. Romans 12:16

6. Choose a verse from this portion of Scripture, and make it your memory verse for this week. Begin working on it today.

DAY 3 – BEGIN IN PRAYER

1. Read 1 Peter 4:10-19.

2. How are we to minister to one another according to verse 10?

How would you define the term **good stewards**?

With whatever God has enabled us, we must serve as **good stewards**. A steward is one who manages someone else's goods. Most people in Peter's day would have understood the concept of stewardship because as slaves they possessed nothing of their own; all they handled belonged to their masters. How does this concept of stewardship apply to the gifts of grace God has given you?

We are to be good stewards of the **manifold grace of God**. Manifold literally means **multi-colored** and it refers to various ways and gifts that God's grace can be found in the Body. We are needed by, and have need for, one another. What specific gifts has the Lord given you? How are you using them?

3. In verse 11 Peter gives us two lessons on our outlook as we set about serving the body. How are we to serve one another, and what is to be our motive?

Read the following accounts of faithful stewardship, and record what you learn from their examples.

    a. Mark 14:3-9

    b. Matthew 25:14-30

4. Why do you think Peter constantly reminds his readers that they are loved?

Many Christians are surprised when trials come into their lives because it is often falsely preached that when we place our faith in Jesus life will be easy. What do the following Scriptures teach us about trials and their purpose?

    a. 1 Corinthians 10:13

    b. 1 Thessalonians 3:2-4

    c. 1 Peter 1:6-8

5. According to 1 Peter 4:13, rather than be surprised by the trials that God allows in our lives, what are we instructed to do?

What will be the outcome of learning to rejoice in our trials?

What more can we learn, and how will it affect how we face the trials God allows?

   a. Luke 6:22, 23

   b. Acts 5:40-42

   c. Romans 5:3-5

   d. James 1:2-4

Personal: Have you been rejoicing in the midst of your trials this week?

6.   Record your memory verse for this week, and spend time committing it to memory today. Remember the importance of hiding God's word in your heart!

DAY 4 – BEGIN IN PRAYER

1.   Read 1 Peter 4:10-19.

2.   When Paul met Jesus on the road to Damascus, the Lord asked him, "Why are you persecuting Me?" Jesus fully identifies with the sufferings of the church and His children. What amazing declaration of faith does Paul make in Philippians 3:8-14?

How can you personally apply this truth in your Christian walk?

What do you count as loss that you may gain Christ?

What "one thing" did Paul determine to do?

3. In verse 13 Peter reminds us to **rejoice to the extent that you partake of Christ's suffering**…and what will happen when His glory is revealed?

What is added in the following Scriptures?

    a. Romans 8:16-18

    b. 2Corinthians 4:17, 18

How do Paul's last words to the elders in Ephesus from Acts 20:22-24 encourage you today?

4. According to 1Peter 4:14, what happens when we are **reproached for the name of Christ**?

How did the apostles respond when they were reproached for the name of Christ in Acts 5:40-42?

What more do we learn about how we must learn to face persecution for Jesus' sake?

    a. Matthew 5:10-12

    b. Hebrews 12:1-3

c. Philippians 1:27-29

5. The word **reproached** in 1 Peter 4:14 means to **chew on with one's teeth**. So when the world turns on you verbally as you speak up for Jesus, be encouraged and know you are blessed for God is at work in your life. However, what warning are we given in verse 15 about suffering for the wrong reasons?

What do you notice about this list of sins that brings deserved suffering?

Suffering brought on by wrong behavior is not profitable to us or to others. Instead it simply brings reproach that has been earned for sin. Yet suffering as a believer is nothing to be ashamed about. What encouragement did Paul send to Timothy in 2 Timothy 1:8?

6. Record your memory verse for this week, and spend time committing it to memory today. Remember the importance of hiding God's word in your heart!

DAY 5 – BEGIN IN PRAYER

1. Read 1 Peter 4:10-19.

2. A truth we must learn fully and stand on completely is that God uses these fiery trials purposefully! He allows them in our lives to cleanse us, to prove us, and finally to use us as a witness to the lost. What assertion does Peter make in verses 17 and 18?

If God allows suffering in the lives of His children, how much more suffering can the enemies of God expect to face when they stand before Him in judgment? What does Proverbs 11:31 tell us about this truth?

3. The righteous ones are scarcely being saved through great difficulty and trouble. What will the unrighteous have to face because of their rejection of the sacrifice of God's Son and the ongoing witness of God's people?

    a. Psalm 1:4-6

    b. Psalm 37:20

    c. Romans 1:18

    d. Jude 1:15

4. The temptations, trials, and hardships that we face as believers are the ONLY judgment we will face. The good news is this is as bad as it gets! Review the truth about these fiery trials in 1 Peter 4:12-14. How will you decide to rejoice today?

5. What conclusion does Peter draw in verse 19?

How do the following truths help you walk in victory today?

    a. Psalm 37:4-6

    b. Psalm 146:5, 6

    c. 2 Timothy 1:12

6. Record your memory verse for this week, and spend time committing it to memory today.

DAY 6 – BEGIN IN PRAYER

1. Spend today reading through the week's lesson and your answers. (It's important!)

2. How has the Lord spoken specifically to you through the lesson this week?

3. What Scripture meant the most to you?

4. Record your memory verse below without looking!

"Adversity is the diamond dust heaven polishes its jewels with!"

Robert Leighton

The Flock and Their Pastors

DAY 1 – BEGIN IN PRAYER

1. Read 1 Peter 1:1-5:6 (Read it as a personal letter written to you. Don't skip this!)

2. Peter writes to the church about its present challenge of persecution, the work of reaching the lost in the process, and the hope that awaits them in the presence of God. Persecution was on the rise. The church was suffering tremendously; therefore, Peter writes with hope and encouragement. Record an important truth you learned from last week's lesson.

How were you able to apply it in your walk this week? Be specific.

3. Read 1 Peter 5:1-6.

4. Is there a warning or a promise? Is there an exhortation or a command?

Select one to apply to your walk with the Lord this week. Which is it?

5. Choose a verse from this portion of Scripture, and make it your memory verse for this week. Begin working on it today.

DAY 2 – BEGIN IN PRAYER

1. Read 1 Peter 5:1-6.

2. In chapter 5 Peter gives us his final words of encouragement about how to walk and to be victorious in the midst of trial and persecution. By submitting our hearts and our lives to the Lord, and to one another, we will find a peace and victory that will sustain us through every hardship. Who does Peter address in verses 1-3?

What are his instructions?

According to Ephesians 4:11-12, what is the specific job of the pastor?

3. Peter speaks to the elders of the church about their attitude and outlook in their ministry and service. The Lord's call to submission within the church also fully applies to pastors and leaders. Use your Dictionary of Bible Words to define the word **elders** in 1 Peter 5:1.

The first mention of the word **elder** in the New Testament is found in Acts 11:30. How do the following Scriptures help define the role of the elder?

a. Acts 14:21-23

b. Acts 15:4-6; 22-31

c. Acts 20:17; 28-32

4. The title **elder** is used throughout the Bible. It can speak of both **age** and **office**, and the usage can be determined in its context. Here in 1 Peter 5:1 the **office** of the elder is the topic. The elder's calling from the Lord is to care for the spiritual well being of the flock. Even though Peter was one of the greatest leaders in the early church, what do you notice about the spirit with which he addresses his fellow elders in verse 1?

How does he describe himself to his readers?

What events in Peter's life may have brought him to this place of humble service amongst the body?

5.   We are all equal, one with another, in the Body of Christ. There is to be no hierarchy within the church. Peter describes himself as a **fellow elder, a witness of the suffering of Christ**, and he looks forward with hope…**a partaker of the glory that will be revealed**. How do the following Scriptures help us walk in hope in spite of trials?

    a. 2Corinthians 5:1-7

    b. Philippians 1:21-24

    c. Colossians 3:1-4

    d. 2Timothy 4:8

6.   Choose a verse from this portion of Scripture, and make it your memory verse for this week. Begin working on it today.

DAY 3 – BEGIN IN PRAYER

1.   Read 1Peter 5:1-6.

2.   What instruction does Peter give to the elder/overseer in verse 2 regarding his care for the flock?

3. The word **shepherd** in verse 2 is **poimaino** in Greek, which means to **feed and tend as sheep**. How is the Greek word translated in Ephesians 4:11?

With the emphasis on feeding, this term **shepherd** is a word that speaks of the total care of the needs of the sheep. The same Greek word is found in John 21:16. What instruction did Jesus give to Peter?

The most vital work of a pastor is to feed the flock of God. What exhortation and warning is found in Hosea 4:6?

What promise does the Lord make to His people in Jeremiah 3:15 regarding their shepherds?

4. Because true shepherds, like David who was a man after God's own heart, are concerned with the welfare of the flock of God, they will feed them His Word. What exhortation and instruction is given to us regarding the crucial importance of God's Word in the life of the believer?

    a. Deuteronomy 8:3

    b. Job 23:12

    c. Jeremiah 15:16

    d. 1 Peter 2:2

5. According to 1 Peter 5:2, to Whom does this flock (the church) belong?

How is the shepherd described in 1 Corinthians 4:1-2? What is required of him?

What happened within the church at Corinth as recorded in 1 Corinthians 3:4-9 because they forgot the eternal truth that the church belongs to God?

6.   Record your memory verse for this week, and spend time committing it to memory today. Remember the importance of hiding God's word in your heart!

DAY 4 – BEGIN IN PRAYER

1.   Read 1 Peter 5:1-6.

2.   The calling of the pastor/shepherd is certainly far more than a vocational choice, more than fulfilling a job description, and more than simply graduating with a diploma. It is a holy calling and a sacred trust from God. It is not to be taken lightly or entered into flippantly. With what heart and motive is the pastor to serve according to verses 2 and 3?

The same Greek word that is translated **compulsion** here is also used in 2 Corinthians 9:7. How is it translated and what does it mean to you?

How is the same word used in Philemon 1:14?

3.   True pastors will continue to feed and disciple the body regardless of the difficulty involved, or the sacrifice required, for God has moved their hearts to serve. Their motive must be love for the Lord and His sheep, never personal for gain or riches. The Greek word for **dishonest gain** speaks of a person out only for himself. In the King James Version it is translated **filthy lucre.** Tragically, this sin within the church has always been a major stumbling block to effectively preaching the Gospel. How did Jesus deal with it in the following Scriptures?

a. John 2:13-16

b. Matthew 21:12, 13

Paul often wrote and warned the elders of this wicked motive. According to 1 Timothy 3:2-7, what are the spiritual qualifications of the bishop (elder, pastor, shepherd)?

4.   Furthermore, the pastor is not to **lord over those entrusted to him**. He is not to serve with pride or for power. He has been given the power to serve the flock and to lead by example. What instruction did Paul give to the elders at Ephesus in Acts 20:28 regarding their care for the church?

Authority can certainly be misused, especially when it is separated from Jesus' example of servanthood. What do we learn from Matthew 20:25-28 regarding the proper motive of leadership?

Read John 13:4-17. By His actions, our Lord gave us the perfect example of the servant leader. What do you learn?

Personal: How are you doing following His example in your service?

5.   Shepherds must lead, correct, establish, and enforce doctrine within the church in a spirit of responsibility and mercy, realizing the sheep belong to the Great Shepherd. What forceful warning is sounded by the Lord through the prophet Ezekiel in Ezekiel 34:2-10?

The pastor **must be an example** to the flock. This Greek word translated **example** means **a model, a stamp or pattern** that others can trace or follow. He must seek to live a life that will bring glory and honor to the Lord and that others can trace or pattern themselves after. What did Paul write to Timothy in 1Timothy 4:12-16?

How does this life of humble servanthood apply to every believer? How will this reminder affect how your serve others today?

6. Record your memory verse for this week, and spend time committing it to memory today. Remember the importance of hiding God's word in your heart!

DAY 5 – BEGIN IN PRAYER

1. Read 1Peter 5:1-6.

2. According to verse 4, what is to be our motivation and hope in serving Jesus?

What do we learn from 2Timothy 4:8?

Personal: Are you longing for His appearing?

3. Remember Peter began chapter 5 by speaking to the elders in the church. What instruction does he give to the Body of Christ in verse 5? To whom are we to submit?

The topic of submission continues to surface in Peter's writings, for by it God accomplishes His work in us and through us. Knowing that the coming of the Lord is near and that the reward to the faithful is imminent ought to cause every believer to submit to the Lord and to the leadership He has set in place. With what are we to be clothed?

4. The elder can certainly provide the younger with the wisdom that experience has brought him; but to be teachable we must be humble. Use a Dictionary of Bible Words to define the word **humility** in verse 5.

What more do we learn about this spiritual characteristic of humility?

    a. Psalm 34:18

    b. Proverbs 15:33

    c. Isaiah 57:15

    d. Colossians 3:12-14

5. To be **clothed in humility** means to be **wrapped in the humility.** This certainly is not a highly valued characteristic in the days we live in. In fact, much of society probably considers humility a weakness. Why ought we be clothed with humility?

Peter is quoting Proverbs 3:34. What does it teach us?

How does James 4:6, 7 speak about this necessary Christian virtue?

How would diligently obeying Romans 12:10 affect the spiritual climate in your church? How about in your home?

Personal: How specifically can you better obey this command?

6.   Record your memory verse for this week, and spend time committing it to memory today.

DAY 6 – BEGIN IN PRAYER

1.   Spend today reading through the week's lesson and your answers. (It's important!)

2.   How has the Lord spoken specifically to you through the lesson this week?

3.   What Scripture meant the most to you?

4.   Record your memory verse below without looking!

Parting Words of Faith and Victory

DAY 1 — BEGIN IN PRAYER

1. Read 1 Peter. (The entire letter.)

2. Peter writes to the church about its present challenge of persecution, the work of reaching the lost, and the hope that awaits them in the presence of God. Persecution was on the rise. The church was suffering tremendously; therefore, Peter writes with hope and encouragement. Record an important truth you learned from last week's lesson.

How were you able to apply it in your walk this week? Be specific.

3. Read 1 Peter 5:7-14.

4. Is there a warning or a promise? Is there an exhortation or a command?

Select one to apply to your walk with the Lord this week. Which is it?

5. Choose a verse from this portion of Scripture, and make it your memory verse for this week. Begin working on it today.

DAY 2 — BEGIN IN PRAYER

1. Read 1 Peter 5:7-14.

2. With the theme of submission still in view, we come to the conclusion of Peter's first letter. The spiritual discipline of submission to God, and to others, develops a humble heart that God can use for His glory. It also delivers us from the pride of heart that God will resist and deal with severely. According to verse 7, what decisive action must we take and why?

Use a Dictionary of Bible Words to define the word **casting** in verse 7.

3.   Your heavenly Father is not unaware of the trials and hardships you face or the difficulty of the path on which He has sent you. The word **casting** means **to throw upon or place upon**. We are to let Him have our concerns; we are to throw them His way and not retrieve them as if we are fishing and reeling in the line. How do the following Scriptures help you in **casting your cares** today?

         a. Psalm 27:13, 14

         b. Psalm 55:22

         c. Hebrews 13:5,6

4.   Two different words are used in verse 7 to give us the English word **care**. The first speaks of anxiety and is from the root of the word for **divide**. It refers to that which divides your attention; to that which distracts you. The worry and concern that occupies our thoughts and our minds divides us from life, and from a walk with God and serving others. According to Philippians 4:6, 7, how can you **cast your cares upon Him**?

The second word **cares** means to take **great concern**. The marvelous truth here is that it is God Who is concerned over His children. What was King David's reaction to this fact in Psalm 8:4-9?

5.   The reality is that most of us are far too familiar with the problem of worry and anxiety. Peter tells us that the solution for fear and anxiety, depression and overwhelming worry is that we must learn to throw every care to the Lord and rest in His care for us. In order to do so, we must know and trust the Lord and His faithfulness. What instructions did Jesus give us that remind us not to worry or fear?

a. Luke 12:22-32

b. Matthew 6:8

We need to learn this two-step process in order to walk in peace and victory. Cast your cares, and rest in His care. **Cast and rest, cast and rest, cast and rest**... Record 1Peter 5:7.

Personal: Read Ephesians 3:20, 21 as a prayer of praise today; will you trust Him with the hardships and concerns in your life today? It will take a determined choice to surrender to His care!

6.   Choose a verse from this portion of Scripture, and make it your memory verse for this week. Begin working on it today.

DAY 3 – BEGIN IN PRAYER

1.   Read 1Peter 5:7-14.

2.   In order to experience victory in Christ Jesus, we must bring every thought into captivity in Jesus Christ. How will obeying the following Scriptures help you to walk in faith in the midst of trial?

a. Isaiah 41:10

b. James 1:5

c. Philippians 4:13

3.   What warning found in 1 Peter 5:8 reminds us that even while we rest in God's care we must be always watchful? Why?

Use a Dictionary of Bible Words to define the following words in verse 8.

   a. Sober

   b. Vigilant

How does verse 8 describe the devil? What is his mission?

4.   Your adversary – the devil – is stalking you like a roaring lion hoping to find someone he can devour. He despises you and sees you as food. In context of this passage, what is one major tool he uses to bring destruction to the life of the believer?

Knowing our enemy's character and mission Peter gives us three important principles for victory. We must respect him, recognize him, and resist him. What do we learn from verses 8 and 9, and how will you apply these truths to your walk today?

We must respect the enemy because he is dangerous. His various names declare his power and evil nature. What is he called?

   a. John 10:10

   b. John 17:15

5. We must recognize his tactics because he is the great pretender, so we need to be vigilant.

    a. John 8:44

    b. 2Corinthians 11:13-15

We must resist the enemy of our faith and stand firm on God's promises in the face of his lies, deceptions, questioning, and taunts. How is this possible?

    a. Ephesians 6:10-13

    b. Romans 8:37

6. Record your memory verse for this week, and spend time committing it to memory today. Remember the importance of hiding God's word in your heart!

DAY 4 – BEGIN IN PRAYER

1. Read 1Peter 5:7-14.

2. We are to stand in faith, as David did before Goliath, trusting in the name of our God. We are to maintain our walks by faith rather than by our own strength. Notice that resisting in faith follows casting all our cares upon Him! How does James 4:7, 8 support this truth?

Before we can stand before Satan we must bow before God. Our enemy roars as a hungry lion, yet we have been given everything we need in Jesus to walk in victory. Record 1 Corinthians 15:57.

What exhortation is given to us in 1 Corinthians 15:58?

3.   What reminder are we given in 1 Peter 5:9 that ought to encourage us when we think no one else has ever suffered like we suffer?

How does 1 Corinthians 10:13 give you confidence in your walk today?

When faced with trial and/or temptation, what is to be your first response?

How will the following truths help you walk victoriously today?

     a. Luke 4:3-13

     b. Hebrews 12:1-3

     c. Ephesians 6:11-13

4.   Peter closes his letter by reminding us once again that God knows what He is doing, He is still in complete control, and that all things have a purpose for good in His hands. How does Peter describe our Heavenly Father in 1 Peter 5:10?

What calling has He placed upon our lives as His children?

Again, what is the purpose of the hardship and trials?

What do we learn from 2Corinthians 4:17, 18 about these trials?

5.   As sons and daughters of the King of Kings, we are being trained daily by the leading of the Holy Spirit. What four terms does Peter use in 1Peter 5:10 to describe God's work in our lives?

Use a Dictionary of Bible Words to define these four words.

1.

2.

3.

4.

Paul, like Peter, was able to write of the hopefulness that he possessed while facing trials. What declaration does he make in Romans 5:3-5?

In thinking about God's eternal plan to mature the saints, Peter wrote a praise chorus. Record 1Peter 5:11 and sing it in your heart today!

6.   Record your memory verse for this week, and spend time committing it to memory today. Remember the importance of hiding God's word in your heart!

DAY 5 – BEGIN IN PRAYER

1. Read 1 Peter 5:7-14.

2. What part did Silvanus play in sending the important letter to the churches?

What was the purpose of the letter?

3. Silvanus is also called Silas. He was one of the chief men in the early church. What do we learn about him from Acts 15:22?

What does Acts 15:32 add?

4. As Peter closes his letter, he no doubt wants to leave exact locations unknown. The early church referred to Rome as Babylon because it was steeped in idolatry. Persecution there was steadily increasing. Where Peter was writing from is unclear, but he sends his greeting from the elect (the church) who dwelt in a hostile world. According to verse 13, who was with Peter as he wrote?

What do we learn about John Mark, Peter's son in the faith, from the following Scriptures?

  a. Acts 12:25

  b. Acts 13:13

  c. 2 Timothy 4:11

5.   Peter encourages his readers to send a warm greeting to the saints. The kiss of love (holy kiss) was cultural in the day of Peter's writing and is mentioned three other times in the New Testament. It is still culturally relative in many countries today. How might we express this warm greeting in our churches today?

Peter opened this letter by wishing his readers peace. Now he closes with the same prayer for them. What do we learn about the source of true peace that will keep us during trials and persecution?

a. Psalm 29:11

b. John 14:27

c. John 16:33

d. Philippians 4:6-9

6.   Record your memory verse for this week, and spend time committing it to memory today.

DAY 6 – BEGIN IN PRAYER

1. Spend today reading through the week's lesson and your answers. (It's important!)

2. How has the Lord spoken specifically to you through the lesson this week?

3. What Scripture meant the most to you?

4. Record your memory verse below without looking!

Made in the USA
Middletown, DE
12 September 2022

10043554R00084